Words in a French Life

LESSONS IN LOVE AND LANGUAGE FROM THE SOUTH OF FRANCE

Kristin Espinasse

A Touchstone Book
Published by Simon & Schuster
New York   London   Toronto   Sydney

TOUCHSTONE
Rockefeller Center
1230 Avenue of the Americas
New York, NY 10020

This Touchstone Edition 2007

TOUCHSTONE and colophon are registered trademarks of Simon & Schuster, Inc.

For information about special discounts for bulk purchases, please contact Simon &
Schuster Special Sales at 1-800-456-6798 or business@simonandschuster.com.

Designed by Joy O'Meara

Manufactured in the United States of America

3 5 7 9 10 8 6 4 2

The Library of Congress has cataloged the hardcover edition as follows:
Espinasse, Kristin, date.
Words in a French life : lessons in love and language from the south of France /
Kristin Espinasse.
p. cm.
1. Americans—France. 2. France—Social life and customs. 3. French language.
I. Title.
DC34.5.A44E77 2006
305.813'044—dc22   2006040457
ISBN-13: 978-0-7432-8728-9
ISBN-10:   0-7432-8728-2
ISBN-13: 978-0-7432-8729-6 (Pbk)
ISBN-10:   0-7432-8729-0 (Pbk)

Portions of this book were originally published in France as part of
Words in a French Life: Volume One copyright © 2004 by Kristin Espinasse, *Words in a
French Life: Volume Two* and *Words in a French Life: Volume Three* copyright © 2005
by Kristin Espinasse. All rights reserved.

For Aunt Charmly and Uncle Tucker,
with love

Introduction

My children have come up with a new game that sends them into fits of laughter. They ask me to say something, *anything,* in their native tongue.

"J'adore la couleur rouge," I love the color red, I say, aware that the kids will have a linguistical one-up-on-mom heyday with all those screaming r's: *adore-rouge-couleur.*

My ten-year-old's face lights up and, with a grin, Max mimics me, *"J'adorrr la couleurrr rrrouge!"* he says, putting a lot of emphasis on the French consonant that I have mispronounced. My son is only teasing me. These days he is more fascinated by my American accent than embarrassed by it.

Next, eight-year-old Jackie gets the spotlight. *"J'adoRRR la couleuRRR RRRouge!"* she says, amused to mimic my unrolled (un-French) "r."

When it's my husband's turn, he pronounces the sentence as he's heard it, further twisting my American accent.

"ZHAH DORRRRR LAH COO-LERRR ROOZH!" he says, batting his eyelashes for effect.

Max and Jackie are now snorting. At this point, I'm holding my stomach as well, and wipe my eyes, laughing louder than even my children. Is my accent really that bad? How could that be? After twelve years living in France and conversing with the French it is as unchanged as the day I stepped off the plane in the Marseilles international airport straight from Arizona, to begin my new French life.

But however imperfectly, I *can* speak French! I can chew out and rattle off; I can small talk, sweet talk, and even talk back; I can crack a joke and, if need be, lay down the law, in a language that once intimidated me to the point of silence.

My love of all things French began sometime around the age of twelve. I don't remember what event preceded it, but I'll never forget my mother telling me, "In your last life, you must've been French!" (This was a remarkable statement considering our religious orientation: though we were born-again we did not believe in reincarnation.) In high school I struggled through French class, receiving below-average grades. Though I loved French words, I did not like French grammar and rules. I still don't.

When I enrolled in the liberal arts program at Arizona State University, I was required to take two years of a foreign language. I gave French another try. A certain French teacher named Madame Wollam—who did not mark up all of my papers in red, but corrected the lesson in question—would forever change my outlook on the language: she assured me that French was something I could eventually understand if I would relax and not get hung up on my weak points vis-à-vis the language. With Mme. Wollam's encouragement, I signed up for an exchange program.

I spent fall semester in Lille, France. For a desert rat from Phoenix, the northern European city could have been an icy French hell. Thankfully, my host family, the Bassimons, provided a warm and welcoming home and I had another wonderful teacher, this time French. Mme. Rudio wrote out all of our grammar lessons in long hand before running them through the copy machine to hand out. It was she who would introduce me for the first time to French expressions, igniting my love for the language.

When fall break, or *les vacances de la Toussaint*, arrived, I joined a classmate and boarded an all-night train. Stepping off the platform in Aix-en-Provence, I knew instantly that the south of France was where I wanted to be—forever. I stood in awe before the puzzle-skinned plane trees that lined an ancient cobblestone boulevard, the lively cafés that spilled out onto the bustling sidewalks, and the moss-covered fountains that acted as commas along an exclamation-packed boulevard.

After less than three months in Lille, fall semester ended and it was time to return home to the desert. While my classmates headed back to Arizona, I found a way to stay on in France, with permission from the department adviser to do an independent study. In exchange for college credit, I wrote about French culture as I had experienced it in Lille and in my new town, Aix, where I had moved. I was just buying time; for what, I did not know. What was sure was that I did not want to leave France. Not yet.

Back in Aix, I was ~~dancing the night away~~ wholly devoted to study when I met my future (French) husband. He barely spoke to me the night we met, but his first words to me—before even *"Bonsoir"*—were *"Il faut qu'on se revoit,"* we must see each other again. His dramatic greeting stopped time. When he handed me his card, I thought I had stepped into the pages of a fairy tale. Beneath his name, "Jean-Marc Espinasse," were the words *"Roy d'Espagne,"* King of Spain.

All that following week, just days before I would return to Phoenix, Jean-Marc and I would rendez-vous for drinks at *Le Grillon* along Aix's historic tree-lined Cours Mirabeau and share spring rolls or *nems* at a Chinese restaurant tucked into a quiet quarter of the city Cézanne once called home. Eager to share his love for the countryside, my royal companion whisked me away to the Provençal hinterland, to where the earth turned red and yellow in the town of Roussillon, and to Gordes, where the houses are made of local rock: souvenirs I would cling to during the separation that loomed before us.

The night before I returned to Phoenix, Jean-Marc's mother welcomed me with open arms at their home in Marseilles, located in an apartment complex known as "Le Roy d'Espagne." Like that, the "title" on the card beneath Jean-Marc's name turned out to be an address. King or not, I had already fallen in love.

The next day I said a teary *au revoir* to Jean-Marc and returned to Tempe to finish my final year of school. We had exchanged phone numbers and addresses, but no promises for the future; those vows had already taken hold somewhere inside of us.

When I graduated with an honors degree in French the following year, ads mentioning "French language a plus" weren't exactly crowding the classifieds in Phoenix, so I seized the first opportunity I could find. I tried my luck as a receptionist for a construction company with ties to France. But the only ties to France it had for me turned out to be opening the mail that was sent from there.

Jean-Marc began to send me postcards of the French countryside. "I still think of you," the first card said. I noticed the dove on the facing side, just above the old blue window shutters. From then on, images of his Provence arrived in my mailbox weekly. Rolling lavender fields, the old stone *cabanon* with its colorful chipped shutters and a valley of sunflowers beckoned; Jean-Marc had thoughtfully penned in messages such as, *"Notre maison?"* our house? next to the warm scenes of country life.

A dozen postcards later, we began talking seriously about a move—*my move*—to France. The plans soon came together and, within a month, I quit my job, packed three cardboard U-Haul boxes, and flew to Marseilles. That October, autumn leaves fell in Provence as I bid adieu to the desert.

Jean-Marc found us an apartment at La Pointe Rouge, an old fishing quarter in the ninth district or *arrondissement* of Marseilles. The windows from our tiny kitchen and living room overlooked the quiet Mediterranean port. Jean-Marc gave me a tour of the neighborhood, pointing out *la boulangerie, l'épicerie* or grocer's, and *la poissonnerie,* where the morning's catch was laid bare on ice, fish eyes intact and glazed over, rows of sharp pearly whites daring one to order.

We checked out the *centre-ville*, speeding through the ancient city on Jean-Marc's Kawasaki. When vehicles backed up, he eased the dirt bike onto the sidewalk and we weaved in and out of pedestrian traffic. My arms circled his waist to temper all the zigzagging and curb hopping and drawing me closer to him.

In addition to helping me with my paperwork to obtain a *carte de séjour*—the official document from the French government giving me the right to reside in France—Jean-Marc found me a job which I began four days after touching down on French dirt. When I told him I did not think I could teach English at the Chamber of Commerce, he assured me, *"Tout va bien se passer,"* everything will go just fine. And it did, for a time.

By Christmas the novelty of setting up house in a foreign country was wearing off. The "playschool" appliances were no longer cute but annoying, the sit-down showers were no longer funky but cramped, room-flooding, and ridiculous, the *mistral* wind no longer exhilarated, it froze and chapped. I began to long for the ease and user-friendliness of my hometown: the wide driving lanes and easy-to-navigate roads, the large washer/dryer combo I had at my last home, drive-through banking, and department stores where you can buy anything from tires to toothpaste.

While I struggled with my homesickness, Jean-Marc had a close-knit circle of friends to call, visit, or invite over when he felt like company or needed moral support. And though he shared them with me, it was not the same. While he was cozy and complete in his French element, I was fronting the blizzard of

Foreign Ways of Being, or French mentality and etiquette. The strange faces ignoring me on the bus each morning did little to comfort, and a yearning for my own friends, family, and home-town grew.

After a series of plate-shattering disagreements we came to the conclusion that things were not working out. Even still, I was deeply disappointed when Jean-Marc took the initiative and drove me to the travel agent's to purchase my one-way ticket home.

Back in Arizona I found a job selling scale-model cars for a small mail-order catalog, which turned out to be the perfect nurse-your-broken-heart job. Isolated and working in an over-air-conditioned office, I had plenty of time to think about my loss and to watch my French life flash before me: the cottage we had moved into just before I left, the weekends spent fishing *oursins,* or sea urchins, along the rocky coastline, and the authen-tic homemade meals we so often shared with his friends and fam-ily. Most of all, I remembered one Frenchman's promise to give me all of the love growing inside him, and how he had, but I hadn't felt confident enough to take it, or was too preoccupied to give it back to him.

Back in Phoenix, I found my friends and family carrying on with their own lives, meeting career goals and/or busy in their own relationships and projects. While they were happy to see me back—*and hey, let's meet for a beer sometime*—they were also occupied, having other fish to fry.

While Phoenix was warm, predictable, and easy to navigate, Marseilles, with its violent winds and uncertain tomorrows now pulsed with life and color within my memory. After two emotionally gray seasons in the Valley of the Sun, I sold my car and told myself I had enough cash to get by in France for six months. I knew the truth was more like three or four. I ignored reason and packed my bags once more.

The tricky part was convincing Jean-Marc that this was the right decision for him, too. But he eventually came around and even welcomed me back with an offer to pick me up at the airport.

I was floored when he asked me to marry him almost as soon as I stepped off that plane. Along with a jittery *"Oui!"* in acceptance of his proposal, I promised myself that I would say "oui" to France, too, and change my attitude completely. I wish I could say my newfound fascination for a country that once stirred my preteen heart came right away, but it didn't. It came soon enough.

My son Max was born exactly one year after I reunited with Jean-Marc. Suddenly, the French were speaking to me. *"Qu'il est beau, votre bébé,"* isn't he beautiful, your baby, complete strangers would say, approaching me, sometimes even tapping my arm to underline their point. The human contact felt good.

By the time Jackie was born, two years and four months after Max, I knew many of the other moms in our small village. We had moved from Marseilles to Saint-Maximin when Jean-Marc made an inspiring career change from accountant to wine sales, following a passionate calling that would bring him back to nature and away from crunching numbers beneath artificial light. I would eventually follow in his tracks, working for a Côtes de

Provence vineyard for three years; there, I began to learn and better appreciate Jean-Marc's *métier*.

As our children learned to speak—eventually correcting my French—I became more aware of their growing language. I learned a new slew of words—French childspeak—like *"bobo," "dodo,"* and *"doudou"* (a hurt, sleeptime, and security blanket). As my children grew, so did my vocabulary. Though they understood and responded to me when I spoke English, occasionally answering back in the same language, they spoke French outside and, increasingly, inside the home.

When my son and daughter entered school, I became even more aware of my longtime love of these French words they were learning, and how they tied in to my everyday life. I even began writing some of them down. I decided to begin a weblog (www.french-word-a-day.com) in which to share my cross-cultural adventures, creating a column called "A Day in a French Life."

I offered readers the option to sign up to receive this daily newsletter, and they began to do so, by the thousands and across the globe, often sending their encouragement and kind wishes—as well as corrections—and, in so doing, helped me to find my writing voice.

My family has taken an active interest in my dream-come-vocation. Often the kids will stop mid-phrase and say, "Do you know this word, Mommy? You might use it for French Word-A-Day." They are also zeroing in on my accent these days. Let's hope they can fix that.

I still make sure to return to the States once a year and I have been lucky to have family visit me here. One of the richest moments in my French life was when my mother came here to heal from a broken hip, only to discover that she had cancer, and ended up staying for more than a year. Her verve and enthusiasm for the French, specifically the village folk, forced me to get out and interact, something I sorely needed to do, having lost touch with village life since we'd moved from Saint-Maximin to a new home in Les Arcs outside of the village center. To this day, villagers stop me on the street, asking for an update on "Jules" as they call her.

While I miss Jules and await her next visit, I thank her for helping me to realize to which continent my heart is now anchored. During an emotional good-bye before leaving France, she released me from her arms, looked into my eyes, and voiced my feelings:

"France is your home now," she said. Embracing Max, Jackie, and Jean-Marc she added, "and *this* is your family."

Words in a
French Life

Abricot

(ah-bree-ko)

noun, masculine

apricot

My *belle-mère* is seated at the kitchen table sorting the baskets of apricots with Jean-Marc. She is wearing a black *maillot de bain*, which is hidden beneath her *paréo*. She has on Christian Dior sunglasses with lenses the size of drink coasters. The glasses remind me of a certain American who popularized this look thirty or so years ago. Around my *belle-mère's* neck rests a strand of little gold balls that make up the classic *collier* from Marseilles.

Last week Jean-Marc, Max, and Jackie picked the *abricotier*. Once all of the apricots from the lower branches were *cueillis*, my son climbed up the tree to liberate the out-of-reach fruit. When the apricots tumbled one by one onto his sister's head, she complained, *"Aïe! Fais attention, Max!"*

Earlier that day, my *belle-mère* had said to me, "I thought they were for decoration, those apricots." She was pointing to the baskets of tiny fruit, the color of which is best described as *jaune orangé*. Either she was teasing me again for not getting around to accomplishing one more domestic chore—in this case, the putting up of fruit, or at least the preparing of it for a pie or fruit salad, before it goes bad—or this year's apricots really do look too perfect to be real.

Back at the table I watch mother and son prepare fruit tarts. Michèle-France is using a traditional *moule à tarte,* while Jean-Marc is working with a casserole dish. Because the casserole is too narrow, Jean-Marc presses the excess dough along the tall walls of the dish. I think about how, if the deep dish tart were a fruit prison, the little halved apricots would have one hell of a time scaling those pastry walls.

This is the first *tarte* Jean-Marc has made since I've known him. Witnessing the complicity between mother and son, I imagine he rolled up his sleeves even as a child, slicing and sampling the fruit as it made its way to the prepared baking dish.

After lunch my *belle-mère* and *moi* remain at the table, enjoying a second slice of apricot pie. As we chat, we squint our eyes and twist our faces. If you happened to be a French *mouche* on the wall, you might get the impression that mother-in-law and *belle-fille* were barely tolerating each other. That is, unless you'd tasted that pie—tart, but tasty—and you'd realize they were sharing a silent rapture.

2

REFERENCES: *la belle-mère* (f) = mother-in-law; *le maillot de bain* (m) = swimsuit; *le paréo* (m) = wraparound skirt; *le collier* (m) = necklace; *un abricotier* (m) = apricot tree; *cueillis (cueillir)* = picked; *Aïe! Fais attention, Max!* = Ouch! Be careful, Max!; *jaune orangé* = yellow-orange-colored; *le moule à tarte* (m) = pie plate; *la mouche* (f) = fly; *la belle-fille* (f) = daughter-in-law

Expression

cueillir des abricots = to pick apricots

Aiguille

(ay-gwee)

noun, feminine

needle

I sat out on the front porch, preparing to mend my son's swim trunks. Barbara said she'd drop by in *un quart d'heure* or so to pick up Max and take him, along with her son, Baptiste, to the beach at Saint-Aygulf. I wanted my ten-year-old to look his best, and the *déchiqueture* on the back left "cheek" of his shorts was complicating my mission.

Settled into the wicker-seated chair, I looked ahead to the two rows of fully blossomed lavender, their pointy violet heads attracting the restless neighborhood bees. I thought about the *goûteux* lavender honey the bees were making, and just how good it would taste right about now in a tall glass of *thé glacé*. Beyond the lavender, a thinning hedge of cypress rippled in a motionless fashion, signaling the occasional passerby. With each shade-shifting wave I set down my sewing and tried to make out which *voisin* was out for a walk.

Returning to my task, I noticed the tear was a complicated one: a V rip (or more precisely, according to my son, *un angle droit*, or right angle), not one of those straight rips that would have been a snap to fix, even for this clumsy *couturière*.

Squeezing my right eye shut, I began to thread the *aiguille. Gagné!* The *fil* slid through the needle's eye, thanks to the newly cut thread with no frayed ends to slam against the needle's sides.

I sewed up one side of the rip, then shifted the swim trunks until the second line was horizontal. When I'd sewn that side up, I sealed the stitches with three knots.

"Fais voir la couture," let's see the stitches, Max said from the doorstep, adding, *"Ça ne se voit pas trop?"* It doesn't show too much?

"I don't think so," I replied, hoping not to draw too much attention to the jagged track.

My son examined the stitches. After a moment he looked up and smiled. "It's the best you can do, and that's good, *maman.*"

Like the lavender honey, so sweet were his words. How forgiving a child is, how willing and generous-natured to see past our imperfect stitches.

REFERENCES: *un quart d'heure* (m) = a quarter of an hour, *la déchiqueture* (f) = tear; *goûteux (goûteuse)* = flavorful; *le thé glacé* (m) = iced tea; *le voisin (la voisine)* = neighbor; *un angle droit* (m) = right angle; *le couturier (la couturière)* = tailor, seamstress; *gagné! (gagner)* = won!; *le fil* (m) = thread; *la maman* (f) = mom

Also

une aiguille de glace = an icicle

une aiguille de pin = a pine needle

Expressions

de fil en aiguille = from thread to needle (one thing leading to another)

une petite/grande aiguille = hour/minute hand (of a clock)

discuter sur des pointes d'aiguilles = to split hairs

passer par le trou d'une aiguille = to accomplish something difficult

faire passer quelqu'un par le trou d'une aiguille = to intimidate someone

chercher une aiguille dans une botte de foin = to look for a needle in a haystack

Alimenter

(ah-lee-mahn-tay)

to feed

The young woman wore a tight black camisole top and flowing white pants. She was olive-skinned and had long brown hair with golden highlights. If this were the States in the seventies, she might be called a fox. In the nineties in France they would call her *canon* (that's *kah-noh*).

On that balmy summer night in Marseilles I sat beside her at a friend's dinner party, sneaking furtive sidelong glances as she ate *bœuf* and *patates*. Her *fourchette* stayed in her left hand and the knife in her right; in this fashion she continued to cut pieces of beef and potato and forked them into her mouth until she had reached the bottom of the *assiette,* at which point she tore a section of bread from the baguette and wiped the plate clean.

"*Vous en voulez encore?*"—would you like more?—the hostess asked.

"*Non, merci*"—no thanks. It was delicious but she'd had enough, she added.

On second thought, she had room to spare. When the cheese platter appeared, she retrieved her knife in anticipation. Pausing over the *plateau de fromages*, she hesitated before the *chèvre*, the Camembert, and the Roquefort. In the end, she sampled a little of each, tearing off another piece of bread for good measure. Every now and then, she would pause to drink some water.

By the time the dessert came out, she was tiring, and yet— "Just a small slice," she said, eyeing the *gâteau*. *"Voilà. Merci!"* That's it. Thank you!

As for the cake—in that went.

Earlier, when I arrived, the hostess had greeted me with a kiss and a comment: *"Tu n'as pas encore retrouvé ta ligne"*—you haven't got your figure back. I held a three-month-old Max in my arms and had a diaper bag slung over my shoulder. Thanks to *l'allaitement maternel,* I had lost the weight I'd put on during *la grossesse,* and then some. Her critique not only perplexed, it pierced.

It was that comment that left me watching the French—not only the *canon,* but also my own French family—and their relation to the verb *alimenter.*

"No, thank you," says Max, who'll be ten years old in May, when I offer a second helping of potato chips. Who can resist more *chips*? It must be that French DNA coursing through his blood, rearing its beret-capped head with a "You're full!" signal.

On a Sunday night, after a two-hour picnic in the Lubéron, my husband asks for tea for dinner. Tea! I give him his liquid meal, and make myself a three-egg frittata, washing it down with a tall glass of milk.

In summertime my *belle-mère* raises her hand—halt!—as I

am about add another spoonful of tabbouleh to her plate. It's hot out and she's lost her appetite, and won't be eating just because it's "time to."

All this watching the French has had its effect on me, and besides losing a few pounds since moving to France, I have a new perspective on eating: food is for filling one's tummy, not one's time; meals are for savoring and for spending time together.

REFERENCES: *canon* = gorgeous; *le bœuf* (m) = beef; *la patate* (f) = potato, spud; *la fourchette* (f) = fork; *l'assiette* (f) = plate; *le plateau de fromages* (m) = cheese plate, cheeseboard; *le chèvre* (m) = goat cheese; *le gâteau* (m) = cake; *l'allaitement maternel* (m) = breast-feeding; *la grossesse* (f) = pregnancy

Expression

alimenter son épouse/époux = to provide maintenance, alimony, for one's wife/husband

Appuyer
(ah-pwee-ay)

to press down

Our mauve-colored Citroën has driver's seat armrests. I fasten my seat belt, then try to get the *accoudoirs* to fold up so that the kids and I can begin our voyage east, to the Nice airport. The idea of "resting" any part of the body while operating a two-ton vehicle that will soon career forward at 140 kilometers per hour seems absurd.

I adjust the *rétroviseurs,* then swing around to see if the kids have buckled their *ceintures de sécurité* before I release the parking brake. *Et c'est parti!* And we're off!

Not five minutes into the drive and the backseat drivers pipe in.

"Maman, tu as grillé un feu rouge!" Max shouts.

I explain to Max that the light in question had a blinking yellow arrow beneath it, and that I have made a legal right turn. *"T'inquiète pas, Max!"*

After a few initial pointers—Jackie reminds me, "Take Nice, *maman,* not Aix!" at the first fork in the road, and Max says,

"*Maman,* take *la voie télépéage!*" referring to the express lane at the tollbooth, the one designated by the illuminated orange *T*— we're on our way.

Though we have the small *télépéage* box attached to the windshield, that magic box that communicates with the toll barrier, telling it to lift its long red-and-white striped arm and let our car pass, we will still pay thirteen euros for the round-trip journey to the airport and back. We'll just pay it at the end of the month, and at a slight discount for being tenacious turn-pikers.

We pass the *sorties* for Fréjus, Mandelieu, Cannes, Mougins, and Antibes before beginning to search for the familiar blue *panneau* with the white airplane that indicates *l'aéroport de Nice.* With the Mediterranean Sea to our right, and ships departing to Corsica and *Afrique* and Italy straight ahead, the drive is always an inspiring one; there's the hope that we'll one day board an ocean liner, or cross the border again soon.

A few kilometers from Cannes, I pass the two-tone (bordeaux/cream) *deuche* put-putting along in the right lane. A line of cars whose front fenders are twisted into one big frown trails behind. "Get a move on!" they seem to grumble. The driver in the *deuche,* a *paysan* with a pipe hanging from the corner of his mouth, remains oblivious to the pressure, his elbow out the window, one arm on the wheel.

The children begin to sing:

Chauffeur, si t'es champion,
Appuie, appuie!

11

'hauffeur, si t'es champion,
Appuie sur le champignon!

I don't understand the *paroles*, partly because I am concentrating on the road, and partly because the words are running together into one great foreign-language blur.

The singing stops abruptly when Jackie screams, *"Regardez! C'est l'avion de papa!"* (Look! It's Daddy's airplane!) The three of us hush and look out the window, to the *ciel*. The rumbling in our stomachs—noon approaching—is replaced by a flute song of butterflies.

By the time we arrive at the airport in Nice, I am more relaxed and therefore able to unravel the French words as my children continue to sing, in French:

Driver, if you're the champion,
Then step, then step!
Driver, if you're the champion,
Then step on the gas!

With that, I smile. Whether you put-put forward in a language or in a driving lane, *ce n'est pas grave.* The foreign words and the impatient drivers will eventually unscramble/scram. And if all else fails, know when to sing.

REFERENCES: *un accoudoir* (m) = an armrest; *le rétroviseur* (m) = rearview mirror; *la ceinture de sécurité* (f) = seat belt; *tu as grillé un feu rouge!* = you ran a red light!; *t'inquiète pas* = don't fret; *la sortie* (f) = exit;

le panneau (m) = sign; *l'aéroport de Nice* (m) = Nice's airport; *l'Afrique* (f) = Africa; *une deuche* (f) = Deux Chevaux, a classic and popular Citroën car with a two-horsepower engine; *le paysan (la paysanne)* = farmer; *la parole* (f) = word; *le ciel* (m) = sky; *ce n'est pas grave* = it isn't important

Expressions

appuyer sur le champignon = to step on the gas
appuyer sur la chanterelle = to harp on

Attendre
(ah-tohn-dr)

to wait for

$\mathcal{I}$ arrived at Saint Antoine de Padoue to find all 185 guests chatting outside the church. In America, the bride arrives after the others are seated—at least that's what I had known from film and televised weddings and from the few ceremonies I had attended.

To the tune of "Here Comes the Bride," *la mariée* demurely enters the church and the audience is hushed in awe. This is the part I had waited for my whole life, but in Marseilles, France, the tradition appeared to be *au contraire*.

Ducking for cover from behind the cab window, I snuck a frustrated peek at the crowd.

"Circle around the block, *s'il vous plaît*." The taxi driver honored my request as I sent "Enter the church!" vibes to the oblivious guests. After several trips around the neighborhood, we returned to discover the courtyard empty.

"They're in! Let's go!" Just as I finished my command, I noticed the priest exiting the seventeenth-century church. Oh, no! I'm in trouble again, was all I could think at that point.

The priest dashed forward and impatiently flagged us in. "You are late!" he said, noticeably irritated. I resisted the urge to explain the cultural confusion and thought back to my last run-in with the father just a few weeks prior.

In order to be married in the church, my French fiancé and I were required to attend marriage counseling. The father in question began to inquire about my religious affiliation. Having difficulty categorizing "born-again Christian," he tried to get me to clarify.

"Do you mean Protestant?"

"Uh, no, I mean, I don't think so," I said.

"Baptist?" he offered.

"Could be," I thought aloud. "Do you have Methodists in France?" I asked, with audible wonder.

The priest shook his bearded chin and stared out the window, perplexed by the multidenominational country I came from. In France much of the population is Catholic, period. I managed to pass whatever theological entrance exam I was being given, for several weeks later I found myself exiting the cab on my way up the cathedral stairs to marry my Frenchman.

The guests were now patiently seated and waiting to hear the bride's affirmative, *"Oui."* Outside the church, the *mistral* wind picked up. Standing before the massive entrance, my mom tried to touch up my makeup but I waved her away, not wanting to upset the priest further.

Suddenly the wind moved in, a current swirling underneath

my sheer muslin veil. Next, the veil flew up and attached itself to the side of the church, with me still hooked to the other end, thanks to hairpins en masse. I was now, effectively, stuck to the church wall.

"Aidez-moi!"—help!—I called, to no one in particular. I could not believe the ridiculous predicament I found myself in.

The priest shook his head again while my mother, grandmother, and sister moved to action, trying to disengage the would-be bride from the church wall.

Finally freed, I gathered what was left of my dignity, laced my right arm through my mom's left, and marched down the aisle flanked by smiling (and some still snickering) Frenchmen. Catholic, born-again, Presbyterian, or other, I was just relieved to be there, no longer stuck outside.

REFERENCES: *la mariée* (f) = bride; *au contraire* = the opposite; *s'il vous plaît* = please

Expressions

attendre son heure = to be patient
attendre sous l'orme = to wait in vain

Aube

(ohb)

noun, feminine

dawn

Eight-year-old Max was up almost as early as I yesterday when he came trotting across the yard and into my *bureau*. My office is now located catercorner to the *maison*, in the annex that Jean-Marc and I had built after too many months sharing a desk in our home's busy entrance hallway. From the north window I can now see the mailman arriving on his lemon yellow scooter, and looking east, just across a patch of grass, I can see the kids' rooms and the goings-on there. Best of all, I no longer receive an icy gust of air up my back each time someone opens the front door in wintertime.

I turned my attention from the morning Internet news to the early riser.

"What's the word for today's piece?" he inquired.

"*Kif-kif,* remember? I told you last night."

"Ahhh . . ." he said, visibly searching for the word's meaning.

"Do you know what that is over there?" he said, pointing to the orange-and-pink horizon beyond my computer screen.

"Le soleil," I responded, happy to know the answer to something.

"Non, c'est l'aube en fait."

Silent now before the growing apricot sun, I warmed to another new French word before whispering thanks to the pajama-clothed sage yawning beside me.

REFERENCES: *le bureau* (m) = office; *la maison* (f) = house; *kif-kif* (from *c'est kif-kif* = it's all the same); *le soleil* (m) = sun; *non, c'est l'aube en fait* = no, it's the break of day, in fact

Also

à l'aube = at dawn, at daybreak
à l'aube de = at the dawn of

Balai

(bal-eh)

noun, masculine

broom

*W*atching *les Marseillais* unwind in the cozy ski resort of Serre Chevalier was no *épreuve,* just a highly agreeable sport for anyone who has ever feared the French were *trop chi-chi* or too reserved.

Near the northern Italian border, Jean-Marc and I joined a group of his childhood pals for an annual get-together in the French Alps. Five teams (organized according to which lodge the participants were camped in) geared up to compete in the wackiest of *défis,* including relays, downhill racing, and ice hockey—all with a twist . . .

From the crowded lodge, flanked by the participants' children and a few of the other nonskiers like myself, I waited for the racers—including my husband—to return and share the details of recent relays.

In one of the races, Jean-Marc tells me, the five teams sped down the mountain *en chenille,* clinging to an elastic cord. A shot of *génépi* (at the start *and* finish lines) cured the *trouillards* but mostly gave the Frenchwomen *la nausée.*

Another *défi* took place at the *patinoire,* where I watched from the comfort (and safety) of the sidelines this time. In this event, brooms replaced hockey sticks and a small rubber ball stood in for a puck. While the ball caused more bruises and bumps than *buts,* the cases of beer, which diminished along with the setting sun, assuaged most of the pain.

When competition heated up, what do you imagine the French did?

Stripped down. Naturally.

Never mind the freezing temperatures; shirts rose, and some even flew off. While the French were mesmerized by their own show—hushing in curiosity or giggling at what they seemed to find risqué—I was mystified by their reaction. For me, this was lukewarm viewing. The French Riviera, where skin is in, was burning hot compared to here. And weren't these people from the south (and the sizzle) anyway?

"Why do you find that so exciting?" I asked the wide-eyed Frenchman to my left. "I mean, all summer long the beach is jam-packed with topless women. What is the big deal about seeing a *torse nu* a few hundred kilometers north?"

"The big deal," my friend replied, "is that *this* is not the beach!"

REFERENCES: *le Marseillais (la Marseillaise)* = person from Marseilles; *une épreuve* (f) = an ordeal, test; *trop* = too; *chi-chi* (pronounced *she-she*) = extremely chic; *un défi* (m) = a challenge; *le chenille* (m) = caterpillar; *en chenille* = in a (looping) file; *le génépi* (m) = a liqueur; *un trouillard (une trouillarde)* = a chicken, coward; *la nausée* (f) = nausea; *la patinoire* (f) = skating rink; *le but* (m) = goal, target; *le torse nu* (m) = bare torso

Also

les balais (informal) = years; *avoir trente balais* = to be
    thirty years old
balayer = to sweep
la voiture-balai = the last car in a line of wedding guests'
    cars (usually with saucepans attached to it)

21

Expressions

du balai! = (get) out!
un coup de balai = a massive employee layoff
passer le balai = to sweep the floor
balayer devant sa porte = to sweep before one's door, to
    correct one's own errors before criticizing another's

Beurk

(*burk* or *beark*)

gross

*M*any French find peanut butter *beurk*.

Some Americans say "Gross!" when they read *suprême de pigeon rôti* on the menu.

My daughter says *"Beurk!"* when I serve *épinards*.

My son says *"Beurk!"* when I quiz him over the girls at school.

Our *lapin,* César, finds his condensed industrial bunny pellets *beurk*.

I say *"Beurk"* when I read the news, so I try to avoid it.

My French husband says *"Beurk"* when he tastes oakey California Chardonnay.

But then, he loves Taco Bell.

REFERENCES: *le pigeon rôti* (m) = roast pigeon; *les épinards* (m, pl) = spinach; *le lapin* (m) = rabbit

Bouffe
(boof)

noun, feminine

grub

$\mathcal{A}$ few days before *les faits,* my husband announces that twelve of his relatives are coming for *déjeuner* on Sunday. He's so relaxed that he fancies a little jog. *"Je vais courir,"* he says, stretching his arms.

"What time are they arriving?"

"En fin de matinée."

En fin de matinée ranks right up there with *en fin d'après-midi* for preciseness, for the exactness of time it relays regarding just when an event will take place on French soil.

I have learned that *en fin de matinée* can be anywhere between elevenish and one-thirtyish.

And that *en fin d'après-midi* can be anywhere from the end of the four o'clock hour to 7 PM–ish.

"Don't worry," my husband says, sensing *la panique.* "Everyone is bringing something!"

I'm not sure how he deduced it is the issue of cooking for everyone on such short notice that worries me the most, but I start with the *bouffe.*

"You don't invite someone over for lunch and then tell them to bring the food!"

"*T'inquiète pas,*" he says simply.

"Well, what should I make for lunch?"

"*Rien!*"

"But I've got to make something . . ."

"Why don't you make cookies then?"

"Because your aunts will bring fruit tarts."

"*Voilà,*" he says, and the way his French lips purse as he begins to draw the word out—*vwaaaaah* with a very abrupt *là!* ending—tells me in one double-syllabled word that the earth will continue to rotate with or without my prepicnic jitters.

Well then. OK. I will worry less, trust more, and jump—or "put myself into the bath," as they say over here. However, I remain curious to see just how one can invite a dozen people over and do absolutely *rien.*

In the end, here's how that happened.

A convoy of cars arrived. The *tantes, oncles, cousins, neveux, grand-mère, frère,* and the *chien* exited the *bagnoles* with smiles as big as the baskets that weighed down their arms.

I waved from the terrace, a crooked *sourire* creeping across my face.

"*Salut!*" I said.

"*Salut!*" They replied.

"*Comment ça va?*"

"Ça va très bien!"

As I smoothed down a cotton *nappe,* one of the cousins pulled out crackers and nuts for the *apéro.* With that, baskets were unhitched, *glacières* unhooked, the food and drinks set forth.

"Du Châteauneuf-du-Pape!" Jean-Marc's uncle announced, offering the wine from his vines.

I looked up to a veritable feast. The offerings continued.

"Du pâté, Jacques?"

"Would you like a sausage, Michèle-France?"

"Sabine, goûte ça!"

"Kristi, come and try Geneviève's tart, the cherries are from our garden. *Attention aux noyaux!"*

We formed two rows separated by the mismatched tables that were connected and camouflaged by a pastiche of Provençal tablecloths. Every once in a while, an olive pit would be catapulted over the side of the terrace to land inside the rosemary hedge below. And just like that, we filled our *ventres* in between chatting and laughing under the *soleil du midi.*

When the time came to pile plates, shake out the *nappes,* and saunter over to the shady olive trees for a siesta (along with half the in-laws), I made a promise to myself to remember this day, and how easily it unfolded, just like the tablecloths.

REFERENCES: *le fait* (m) = event; *le déjeuner* (m) = lunch; *je vais courir* = I'm going for a run; *en fin de matinée* = late morning; *en fin d'après-midi* = late afternoon; *la panique* (f) = panic; *rien* = nothing; *une tante* (f) = aunt; *un oncle* (m) = uncle; *le cousin (la cousine)* = cousin; *un neveu* (m)

= nephew; *une grand-mère* (f) = grandmother; *un frère* (m) = brother; *le chien* (m) = dog; *une bagnole* (slang) (f) = jalopy, car; *le sourire* (m) = smile; *salut!* = hello; *comment ça va?* = how are you?; *ça va très bien* = I am fine; *une nappe* (f) = tablecloth; *un apéro* (m) = aperitif; *une glacière* (f) = cooler; *goûte ça (goûter)* = taste that; *attention aux noyaux* = watch out for the pits; *un ventre* (m) = stomach; *le soleil du midi* (m) = afternoon sun

Bouquiner

(boo-kee-nay)

to read (informal)

"Why don't you read in French?" my French friends asked. "*Tiens, prends ça!*" they offered.

One friend gave me her Mary Higgins Clarks—translated into *français;* another, her French *livres de poche.* An Anglophone neighbor delivered a crate of books. "Can you believe someone would throw these out? They're all in French. I thought you might like them."

I looked through the discarded books: some very, very old, some *très, très* pink, as in the *romans roses,* or "pink novels," from the early twentieth century. I sometimes wonder if the name comes from the way French cheeks used to blush when reading the risqué passages. Not being in the mood for the French equivalent of a Harlequin romance, I added the editions to my bookshelf for safekeeping.

My husband then gave me a copy of Nancy Huston's *L'em-*

preinte de l'ange. I paused to admire its *couverture:* a sixteenth-century drawing by Raphael titled *Un Ange.*

"*Merci!*" I said, and displayed the book on my nightstand, where it copied its literary neighbors by collecting *poussière.* They were tempting, but I still wouldn't read them. What's the point of reading an English book that's been translated into French? I reasoned. When cornered, I'd say, "Reading is supposed to be a leisure activity. I can't relax when I am looking up words. Pff!"

My neighbor insisted I sign up at the library. He and his wife drove with me to Saint-Raphaël and stood witness as I received my first French library card. I promptly checked out five picture books.

And then, the *déclic.* I was reading an online review for Maupassant's *Bel-Ami,* fully intent on ordering the English translation, when I stumbled upon a very passionate review. The reviewer had taken the time to urge shoppers to read the book in French, insisting that the English translation would not do the book justice. As impossible as that sounded to me at the time, to read Maupassant in French, I ordered the book.

"I'm reading Maupassant!" I tell people now. Bragging not like a connoisseur who says, "I'm drinking Châteauneuf-du-Pape these days," but like a three-year-old who screams: "I can ride!" Never mind that the bike has training wheels.

Now, words pop off the page like sizzling fireworks and no longer like little language snipers, waiting to undermine my efforts to read in French. The French words roll around my tongue like a caramel, until they melt, but not before infusing my palate with their sound, for I am already whispering the words.

I'm also reading Anna Gavalda's *Ensemble, c'est tout,* and learning *français courant*—the language people use today. When I come across a word I want to remember, like the French word for "crazy," which is *fofolle*—don't you just want to say it?—I close my eyes and repeat, "I *will* remember you! *Fo-folle . . . fo-folle . . . fo-folle.* I *will* remember you!"

As Erik Orsenna has been teaching me in his *La Grammaire est une chanson douce,* "the French language is your country. Learn it. Invent it. It will be, for all your life, your most treasured friend."

REFERENCES: *tiens, prends ça!* = here, take this!; *le français* (m) = French; *un livre de poche* (m) a paperback book; *très, très* = very, very; *un roman rose* (lit.: pink novel) (m) = a romance novel; *une couverture* (f) = cover; *la poussière* (f) = dust; *le déclic* (m) = the trigger

Also

un bouquin = a book
un(une) bouquiniste = a secondhand bookseller

Expression

bouquiner un livre = to read a book

Bourgeon

(boor-zhon)

noun, masculine

bud

After a winter spent mostly indoors behind a computer screen, I took a bit of inspiration from the flowering wild almond trees outside my window. "Spring from your cozy capsule," they whispered; "shoot forth and grow." And like that, on Thursday I shot out of the house, hitching a ride north with Jean-Marc. As the gastronomic restaurants prepare to open for the season, Jean-Marc is making the rounds, proposing his newly composed wine list. When I learned that these places were in the vicinity, I asked if I could come along for the ride, and take in some new sights.

We followed the sinewy path to the town of La Motte, to the stone bridge and over the Narturby, which runs through the charming town. I noticed a row of village homes perched above the river and thought about how nice it would be to live in proximity to such rolling, rushing-over-*les-galets* sound.

The last *virage* had us turning out of town and heading toward the Grand Canyon of the Verdon, the Gorges du Verdon. Sleepy beige fields flanked the two-lane path before us; now and again a lone *cabanon* would appear. Often the crumbling stone sheds have a tree growing from their center, the roof having collapsed long ago.

Here in Provence, there is still not a lot of color in the *paysage* apart from the pastel *volets,* many of which are on their last hinge. The *coquelicots* will rest another month or two before stretching their lovely red arms to the sky, while the *boutons d'or,* or "gold buttons," have just revealed their wrinkly yellow faces; more wildflowers will be up in a matter of days. As for the trees, the *amandiers sauvages* continue to burgeon, with little white puffs exploding like popcorn all over the Var.

That's when the sniffing began.

"That is what you are allergic to!" Jean-Marc said as we approached a line of mile-high cypress trees. (Later he would shake one of the trees, releasing a dull yellow cloud, and point to the dusty, sneeze-producing powder.)

Pulling into the Gorges de Pennafort employee parking, I am drawn to the immense *étang,* where a half dozen swans glide across the calm surface to greet us. At the back of the pond, and somewhat hidden, there is a demure *bastide.*

I stood at the edge of the water, atop a neat green turf, sniffing and sneezing, Kleenex bursting from my pockets.

"*Tu viens?*"—are you coming?—Jean-Marc asked. I tripped over my unlaced shoes as I backed up to snap photos of the swans.

"Yes!" I said, shoving the tissues back into my pockets, out of

31

view, and pushing up my glasses, which kept falling down my nose with each sneeze. I trotted across the grass, Kleenex, camera, glasses, and shoelaces aflutter, to the iron gate, feeling more like a geeky little sister tagalong and not a mature American wife tagalong.

Ça ne fait rien, I reminded myself. The important thing is to bud. To shoot forth and discover.

REFERENCES: *le galet* (m) = pebble; *le virage* (m) = bend; *le cabanon* (m) = shed; *le paysage* (m) = landscape, scenery; *le volet* (m) = shutter; *le coquelicot* (m) = poppy; *un amandier sauvage* (m) = wild almond tree; *un étang* (m) = pond; *la bastide* (f) = country house in southern France; *ça ne fait rien* = it doesn't matter

Also

le bourgeon gustatif = taste bud

Bout

(boo)

noun, masculine

bit

I'm at the cold cuts counter at Super U, hands on hips, tapping feet. The *dame* before me is chatting with the *bouchère* about *tout et rien* until I clear my throat, at which point she pauses, only to continue her *bavardage*.

C'est à nous. The *bouchère* offers Jackie a *gigantesque* slice of salami. The *bouchère* takes her time, carefully pulling off the transparent string of wrapper and rolling the salami to complement six-year-old fingers. *"Voilà!"* she says.

"How's your son?" she asks, ignoring the line behind me. My son? She must have seen us here before. The sides of my lips turn up, in response to her thoughtfulness.

"Don't worry, I won't fool you again," she says, shaking a rump of ham through the air.

And then I remember the practical joke. A few weeks back, I

had left Max at the cold cuts counter after telling him to choose an assortment of *fromages* while I went to get some Choco Pops for our *petit déjeuner*. When I returned, the *bouchère* handed me a one-kilo block of cheese—weighed, wrapped, and ready to go. Rather than hand it back, explaining there had been a mistake, I began fretting about how I'd divide the cheese and freeze it; how we'd have cheese sandwiches for lunch, fondue for dinner, three-cheese pizza (only with Emmental, Emmental, and Emmental). . . . When I looked up, my son and the *bouchère* were laughing. *"Vous m'avez eue!"* I had said. You got me!

I notice her necklace, a chunky clay heart with a rainbow of paint globs. She is a *maman,* I think to myself, because I have the same necklace—Max made it for me in *maternelle.* She is wearing turquoise eyeliner and red lipstick, which match the verve and freshness of her spirit.

"Would you be interested in this last *bout*?" she says, pointing to the heel of the salami. She wants to give me salami! I perk up. *"Oui."*

I am moved as I watch her carefully wrap my *cadeau;* she has remembered me and even thought to give me something. I am ashamed that it has taken a practical joke *and a gift* in order for me to stop to consider her.

Across the store at the checkout counter, I pay for the groceries. As I hand over my *carte de crédit,* I see the *bouchère* leaving the store in civilian clothes. I feel happy that she is off work, away from the frowners in line. I find myself wondering if she is tired, and where she is headed. Off, I imagine, to turn a few more lips right side up.

34

REFERENCES: *la dame* (f) = the lady; *une bouchère* (f) = female butcher or butcher's wife; *tout et rien* = everything and nothing; *le bavardage* (m) = chatting; *c'est à nous* = it's our turn; *gigantesque* = gigantic; *le fromage* (m) = cheese; *le petit déjeuner* (m) = breakfast; one kilo = 2.2 pounds; *la maternelle* (f) = kindergarten; *le cadeau* (m) = gift; *une carte de crédit* (f) = credit card

Expressions

un bout de temps = a little while

faire un bout de chemin = to go part of the way

d'un bout à l'autre = from one end to the other

au bout de la rue = at the end of the street

au bout d'un moment = after a while

au bout du compte = all things considered

au bout du fil = on the other end (of a telephone)

à bout de forces = exhausted

à bout de souffle = out of breath

à bout de bras = at arm's length

joindre les deux bouts = to make ends meet

pousser quelqu'un à bout = to push somebody too far

venir à bout de = to succeed

voir le bout du tunnel = to see the light at the end of the tunnel

Cadeau

(kah-doh)

noun, masculine

gift

$\mathcal{M}$y husband returned home for lunch yesterday bearing a gift. He pulled from his briefcase a small bundle, carefully peeling back the paper towel wrapping.

"C'est un cadeau," he explained. Apparently some business associates had offered it to him.

With thumb and forefinger he lifted out what looked to be a clump of dirt. On closer look, I recognized it as a truffle. *"Une demi-truffe,"* Jean-Marc whispered. Not long ago, if you had told me the gumball-size object was a truffle, I'd have sunk my two front teeth into the side, leaving a nice *morsure* and wincing when the taste of cocoa failed to register.

Jean-Marc selected a plastic container from the *placard* above the sink and set about storing the unexpected gift.

"On a des œufs?" he wondered. Sadly, we had no eggs with

which to make a heavenly truffle-infused omelet. He tucked the truffle safely away into the *frigo* and we sat down for the *repas*.

Later that day I snuck into the *frigo* to observe the little clump—but when I had finished, I guess I hadn't sealed the plastic lid back to the way it was. . . .

Returning to the refrigerator an hour later for another peek, I opened the door on Truffleville. The yogurt smelled and tasted of truffle, as did the bread, the cheese, the lettuce, the tangerines, the *crème-fraîche*, the tapenade, and even the ham . . . *le tout!* Well, I thought, if we had paid the twelve or so euros for that truffle at a supermarket, we certainly would have gotten our money's worth! And besides, tangerines with a truffle flavor are not half bad.

REFERENCES: *c'est un cadeau* = it's a gift; *une demi-truffe* (f) = half-truffle; *une morsure* (f) = bite; *le placard* (m) = cupboard; *un œuf* (m) = egg; *le frigo* (frigidaire, m) = fridge (refrigerator); *le repas* (m) = meal; *la crème-fraîche* (f) = sour cream; *le tout* (m) = everything

37

Expressions

un cadeau publicitaire = a gift, giveaway (product promotion)

un cadeau empoisonné = a gift that is more a curse than a blessing

ne pas faire de cadeau = to not let off lightly

Casse-Croûte

(kass-kroot)

noun, masculine

snack

The good thing about a French picnic is the absence of a table. After all, when it comes to manners, and getting them right, it's all about the table, *n'est-ce pas?* Without that four-legged etiquette foiler, dining in dignity among the French is, well, a picnic.

The biggest *faux pas* visitors to France make is of the hands-in-the-lap genre. While in some countries it is polite to keep one hand in the lap while dining, in France *les mains* should remain *sur la table.* French reasoning goes like this: If you can't see your table mate's hands, you can't be sure just where they are. *Suffisamment dit.*

Lakeside in Lyons, with towels spread out over a bed of pine needles, we sat around the buffet-on-blanket. My friend Nicole unpacked a stack of featherlight wooden bowls before spooning a thick eggplant purée—which she called "Mtabal"—into each *assiette*. With a tear of baguette, we finished part one of the entrée.

Next, Nicole's husband, Michou, passed around a plate of pâté. The first and second courses were followed by homemade tabbouleh, its crunchy mint leaves opening up our palates for more savories to come. Vine-ripe tomatoes were distributed and eaten like apples before a chilled herb-marinated pork roast surfaced from the picnic basket.

When I complimented Nicole on the colorful cups she'd brought along, enabling us to picnic in style, she replied: "It's *too-pehr-waar!*"

Now what could be more delightful at a Frencher-than-French picnic than hearing the French pronounce "Tupperware"?

REFERENCES: *n'est-ce pas?* = isn't that right?; *le faux pas* (m) = false step, or gaffe; *la main* (f) = hand; *sur la table* = on the table; *suffisamment dit* = enough said

Expression

emporter un petit casse-croûte = to take along a bite to eat

Catin

(ka-tan)

noun, feminine

prostitute

Sometimes I smell licorice, sometimes candy . . . the scent of cotton candy, strangely enough. The odors of the *garrigue* are as varied as its wildflowers, which are withering away from the heat.

I love to walk through the aromatic bath of the countryside each evening. It is the herbal scent that draws me out each night, to *balader* along the gravel path behind our home. It is still light out, *l'humidité tombe,* and the air is more pungent: thyme, rosemary, sage, and pine perfume the atmosphere in a kingdom of plants that I cannot name.

I'm a quarter of the way along the dirt path when I cross the *apiculteur.* The beekeeper looks up. *"Bonsoir, madame. Vous marchez?"*

Ben, oui—as a matter of fact—I think to myself, slightly irritated and always confused by the inquiry, which comes every time

I'm out for a stroll. The French can't seem to help themselves.

I pass a man, his wife, and their black poodle. *"Vous marchez?"* they say. The way they ask this question makes me feel like I'm some sort of wanton streetwalker—*une catin!*

As I surface from the woods, my neighbor slows her car, rolls down the window, and looks at me suspiciously. *"Qu'est-ce que tu fais? Tu marches dans la forêt?"* (What are you doing? Are you walking through the forest?) As if the forest behind my home is the Bois de Boulogne, where women, or the *belles-de-nuit,* are known to saunter about late at night. This isn't Paris!

Besides, everyone knows *les putes* from around here hang out on the RN7, the highway just out of town, and not in the *garrigue.* They park along the side of the road, their left leg draped out the side of the car, a camper hooked to the back. I didn't believe it myself, the first time I saw the setup. But it's true. The other girls, from *l'Europe de l'Est,* cluster suggestively under the Provençal pines, wearing hooped earrings and short shorts. With a hip sway in their gait, the women approach the impulsive buyers on wheels who've just careened off the road in a split-second decision for lust.

Back at the *garrigue,* I try to figure out why walking the dirt path is such a novel thing for a woman to do. I begin to observe, noting that the other women who use the path either have a dog or are walking in groups. Sometimes they carry *paniers* to collect wild asparagus or mushrooms. The only other solo women are either jogging or biking. One woman passes on a tractor on her way to tend the vines below.

I don't like to run because the feeling is jarring to me and, as a Frenchwoman told me recently, symbolic of running away (whereas walking is "advancing" in life). A bike is out of the question—it hurts the *fesses*—and a tractor, besides the noise and scent-blocking exhaust . . . *c'est hors du budget!*

The only solution then is to don a *chapeau*. After all, have you ever seen a *catin* in a straw hat?

REFERENCES: *la garrigue* (f) = wild scrubland; *balader* = to stroll; *l'humidité* (f) *tombe (tomber)* = humidity falls; *un apiculteur (une apicultrice)* = beekeeper; *Bonsoir, madame. Vous marchez?* = Good evening, Ma'am. You're walking?; *ben* (not *bien* in this example) (slang) = well, er; *les belles-de-nuit* (f) = beauties of the night (= hookers); *une pute* (f) = hooker; *l'Europe* (f) *de l'Est* = Eastern Europe; *un panier* (m) = basket; *les fesses* (f) = buttocks; *c'est hors du budget* = it's out of the budget; *un chapeau* (m) = hat

Citrouille

(see-troo-y)

noun, feminine

pumpkin

While you won't find parking lots full of faux pumpkin patches here in Provence as you would in the States, the French are catching on to Halloween. The younger generations have begun celebrating *le trente-et-un* with their children, though door-to-door trick-or-treating still calls for some organization (namely, letting the older generations in on things—candy distribution and so forth—via a flyer in the mailbox). That said, the only carved pumpkin I've seen in our neighborhood is *chez nous*, scowling from the mantel of our *cheminée*.

Even our city council has warmed to the ghoulish *fête*. Should you make a small *périple* through our village this weekend, you might just gasp at the sight of so many pint-sized Frenchmen with fangs, phantoms *qui font peur*, and flocks of giggling green-haired *sorcières*. The *mairie* has once again organized *Ah-lo-een*. The *enfants* will parade down the main boulevard, stopping in to each shop to demand some *friandises*.

While it is reported that the most popular Halloween costumes in the States include Spider-Man, SpongeBob SquarePants, and Power Rangers, the French kids will stick with the classics.

At our village *supermarché*, Max, Jackie, and I spent forty-five minutes in the costume department. We were trying to decide if we wanted to be a witch, Dracula, or a monster—the three costumes available—but oh what fretting and hesitation ensued! Max chose a malleable monster mask, and Jackie selected the collapsible coned hat with fake green hair trailing from its base. I hesitated over the Dracula ensemble, but ended up with the monster mask.

44

On the ride home from the market, Jackie, concerned about the limited costume supplies, said to her brother, "There are going to be a lot of other monsters at the party!"

"Don't worry, Jackie, *le tout, c'est de faire peur!*" the most important thing is to scare (people).

A few Halloweens ago, a French mom in our neighborhood organized a trick-or-treat outing. The French kids inserted fangs, attached elaborate tubes that circulated fake blood from the head to the neck, and put on those hideous caps with hatchets attached. Meanwhile the neighbors waited behind closed *portes*, *bonbons* in hand.

Most of the *voisins* showed enthusiasm toward the foreign celebration, though one elderly woman "made grimace soup," shouting at us, *"Allez-vous-en!"* (I think she was just scared, or thought we were some kind of cult.) The rest of the neighbors simply looked at us as if we had two heads. Come to think of it, some of us did!

REFERENCES: *le trente-et-un* = thirty-first; *chez nous* = at our place; *une cheminée* (f) = fireplace; *la fête* (f) = celebration; *un périple* (m) = journey; *qui font peur* = that scare; *une sorcière* = witch; *la mairie* (f) = town hall; *Ah-lo-een* = French pronunciation of Halloween; *les enfants* (m, pl) = children; *une friandise* (f) = bonbon, candy; *le supermarché* (m) = supermarket; *le tout, c'est de faire peur!* = the most important thing is to scare (them)!; *une porte* (f) = a door; *le voisin (la voisine)* = neighbor; make grimace soup (from *faire la soupe à la grimace* = to become angry); *allez-vous-en!* = get out of here!

Expressions

n'avoir rien dans la citrouille = to be empty-headed, bird-brained

avoir un cœur de citrouille = to have a pumpkin heart, to lack stamina

avoir la tête comme une citrouille = to have a pumpkin head, to have a migraine (or a head that feels swollen from information overload)

Cloche

(klowsh)

noun, feminine

bell

In the twelve years since moving to France I had never heard about the *cloches* tradition at Easter. I'd never heard of *les rameaux* either, but then, I'd never attended church over here, apart from weddings and baptismal services.

On Sunday my friend Barbara picked Max and me up for Dimanche des Rameaux (Palm Sunday). Barbara had suggested I collect a few olive or *laurier* branches from our garden and bring them along, which I did.

She pulled her car in front of the *boulangerie*. "Watch this," she said to the kids, managing to parallel park into the tiny space before the baker's. "*Oh-là-là,*" the boys joked, mock-pretending respect for her skill behind the wheel, dropping two sets of jaws for effect.

Next, we headed *à pied* to the *presbytère*, where our sons attend weekly *caté*.

"What's this with the bells at Easter—isn't it supposed to be bells at Christmas?" I asked. "And don't you have an Easter Bunny over here?"

"In France it is the *cloches* that bring the eggs in from Rome," Barbara replied.

Apparently the church bells quit ringing on Good Friday, when the bells fly off for Rome, to return bearing eggs. Three days later the children run out to the garden to watch for the bells, and while they are distracted watching the sky, French parents hide the colorful eggs and chocolates in the garden.

I tried to imagine an inanimate object flying through the air, laden with eggs, but was not satisfied with the image.

"But a *cloche* is a thing! Why are the *cloches* hiding the eggs?"

"*Je ne sais pas.* I think it is a way of incorporating the church into things."

Thankfully, Barbara did not question the absurdity of the Easter Bunny, and we walked on.

Arriving at the *presbytère,* we prepared to have our branches blessed by the *père.* We stood so far back that I worried my *rameau* wasn't receiving any sprinkling of the holy water. *Tant pis.* From the *presbytère* we followed the children and the father down the gravel path and into the church. Unfamiliar with Catholic ceremony, I paid close attention to other churchgoers in order to know what to do next. I tried to understand the sermon, but the father's words resonated off the stone walls, and the French words returned to my ears garbled.

47

• • •

The next night I found myself headed back to church. I parked in front of the *boulangerie*. "Watch this!" I said to Jackie and Max as I angled into the parking space. I had a bit more difficulty parking than Barbara, and when I looked over my shoulder the man in the car behind me was clapping his hands, only the look on his face was not an amused one.

At the *église* the father explained that Pâques meant "passage," and the meaning sent me into reflection. Whereas one week before I'd gaffed my way through mass, singing "Rosanna" instead of "Hosanna," dropping to my knees to pray when the others stood, along with a few other *désastres*, this week was going better.

The past twelve years in France have been a passage, with many faux pas along the cobblestone path. I am learning, this late into the journey, to ask more questions and to listen. I'm learning that we are forgiven for flubbing up holy names (and French words) and that we need not drop or question too closely the traditions that we have brought with us from back home. The Easter Bunny will continue to deliver the eggs at our Franco-American home; as for the bells—they belong with the reindeers, *n'est-ce pas?*

REFERENCES: *le rameau* (m) = branch (olive); *le laurier* (m) = laurel tree; *la boulangerie* (f) = bakery; *à pied* = on foot; *presbytère* = rectory; *le caté* (abbreviation) = catechism; *je ne sais pas* = I don't know; *le père* (m) = father; *tant pis* = too bad; *une église* (f) = church; *le désastre* (m) = disaster

Expressions

déménager à la cloche des bois = to move (homes) without giving notice

Quelle cloche! = What an imbecile!

sonner les cloches à quelqu'un = to strongly reproach someone

se taper la cloche = to eat lavishly

49

Complicité

(kohn-plee-see-tay)

noun, feminine

closeness, complicity

When I was in college, I sold lingerie at Dillard's department store in Phoenix, Arizona. It was a summer job and I was saving for an upcoming exchange program in Lille, France. I was only half present at that job, my mind swirling the rest of the time with the thrilling voyage to be. I was about to embark on what would be a life-changing adventure, and I knew only the part of it then.

I had a onetime customer, a certain Madame Richard (pronounced *rhee-shar*). She had some sort of connection with France, I wasn't sure what, but I'd have liked her despite this fact. It was her eccentricity that charmed me as well as her command of language—both English and French.

She was a woman of a certain age who wore a felt fedora. She was larger than life, and I tried desperately to imagine her story; perhaps she was an *écrivaine* from Paris, or an *artiste*?

She came to Dillard's that day looking for a girdle. I wasn't sure exactly what a girdle was, let alone how to sell her one, but before I could panic she pointed to a distant rack, beyond the string underwear and half-cupped bras, beyond the women's boxers and tanks, beyond the Cross Your Hearts. We headed over to search for the girdle, chatting all the while about *la France* and our passion for all things French, especially the language. We paused briefly to commiserate about stomach paunch and puckered thighs before swooning once again over Paris. Madame ended up with a purchase and was then sadly on her way.

A few days later I was summoned to the department store manager's office. I couldn't imagine the *bêtise* I had committed, but figured I had only another week to go before leaving the job anyway, so I tried to stay calm. The manager handed me an envelope, which I took, noting the fancy lettering; on closer look I recognized Madame Richard's name. The thick linen card inside was colored in navy blue ink, where she kindly stated her appreciation for the *soucis* of a certain employee. The manager then carefully handed me a book, its spine worn through, the title read *La Deuxième Année de Grammaire*.

Inside, the grammar book was inscribed, "A. Richard. Paris 1918."

REFERENCES: *un écrivain (une écrivaine)* = writer; *la bêtise* (f) = stupid thing; *le souci* (m) = care

· ·

Expressions

agir en complicité avec = to act in complicity with

accusé de complicité de vol = accused of aiding and abet-
ting a theft

· ·

Comprendre
(kohn-prahndr)

to understand

*I*n the car on the way home from Décathlon, France's popular sports supply store, I shouted over my shoulder to Max: "No more *pieds nus* in your tennis shoes, OK? You've got to take care of those feet! Remember, only clean feet into clean socks into clean shoes, 'K?"

"She said '*nuls*,' Max!" Jackie shouted, hoping to irritate her brother.

"No, I didn't. I said '*nus*'!" I replied, in my defense.

"She said '*nuls*,'" Jackie continued, ignoring me and baiting her soccer-playing brother. "Your *pieds* are *nuls!*"

While *nul* means either useless or hopeless and *nu* means bare, what was sure was that my daughter was teasing her brother *and* reveling in my faulty French accent.

For once, Max was not irritated by his six-year-old sister. "Just because she's not French," he said, pointing his nose toward the driver, "doesn't mean she doesn't understand stuff, Jackie."

Mon héro.

REFERENCE: *les pieds nus* (m) = bare feet

Expressions

comprendre à demi-mot = to take the hint

comprendre vite = to catch on fast (to understand quickly)

C'est à n'y rien comprendre! = It's completely baffling!

n'y comprendre goutte = to be all at sea, to not understand a thing

Comptoir

(kohn-twar)

noun, masculine

counter

At the Brûlerie Varoise, one of the oldest family-owned *épiceries* in Draguignan, I stood in awe before the canned goods/conserves section: *soupe de poisson, thon à l'huile, pâté de lapin.* . . . I was next in line, and as we were only two clients, I relaxed and perused the *magasin.*

The door rattled and in came a lady with a blue hue in her silver hair and a *charette,* one of those French carts with rollers beneath. The store being a bit cramped with specialty foods, she was obliged to squeeze past a display of *tisane* pots to enter the shop. Almost simultaneously, another lady arrived, with a similar cart on wheels. I kid you not, before she could worry about closing the door, a third woman pushed in, ditto for the cart but minus the blue hue.

By now I was flattened up against a row of tinned *anchois,* thinking the women would not dare ignore me and begin their orders.

Quelle naïveté!

The *dames* clambered to the *comptoir,* the wheels of their carts tangling to a standstill. Despite the distance, they ordered their groceries from afar and above my head, directing the shop owner for Gruyère, *jambon,* and sliced fresh butter from a great slab just next to the cash register.

I stuck out my leg, inching over one of the carts, and grabbing on to the shelf of lavender-tinted sugar cubes, intent on defending *ma place.*

As I skimmed past the pyramid of *bonbons* in a panicked state, the lady behind the *comptoir* met my eyes, directed a warm smile my way, and said above the orders being hollered around me, *"À vous, madame."*

REFERENCES: *une épicerie* (f) = a grocer's shop; Draguignan = French city in the Var region; *la soupe de poisson* (f) = fish soup; *le thon à l'huile* (m) = tuna in oil; *le pâté de lapin* (m) = rabbit pâté; *le magasin* (m) = store; *une tisane* (f) = infusion made of a variety of herbs; *un anchois* (m) = an anchovy; *le jambon* (m) = ham; *la place* (f) = place; *un bonbon* (m) = a piece of candy; *à vous, madame* = your turn, Madam

Cortège

(kor-tezh)

noun, masculine

procession

*F*our moms, eleven kids, and sixteen wheels: a carpool in America, a *cortège de mamans-au-volant* in France.

We looped through the countryside *à la queue leu leu,* en route to Max's basketball match, the road before us flanked by vineyards, wild herbs of Provence, and the occasional *mouton.* We were headed for Lorgues, via Tarradeau, to beat the *chaussettes* off the other team.

I had three supposed *basketteurs* with me, but their real talent, their favorite sport of sports, was backseat driving.

"*Maman,* why are you going this way? Put your *clignotant* on! Where are your glasses?" A barrage of commands spewed forth with the revving of the car's engine. As usual, I spoke in English, the kids in French.

"Quiet! I'm trying to concentrate!"

"What'd she say?" Max's friend asked.

"That we gotta be quiet," Max explained.

"Hey! Don't drink all that water before the game!" I warned them.

"What'd she say now?" the friend wanted to know.

"To go easy on the water."

"Quit—talking—so—loud! I'm trying to drive!"

"And that time?"

"She said for us to shut up."

"I did *not* say shut up; I said, *'Please* be quiet back there!'"

And on it went. You'd have thought they were on the *métro* and my comments were feeding in through a one-way speaker or something.

Exasperated, I left the chatterboxes to chat and turned my attention elsewhere. Taradeau is known for its heavenly goat's cheese, and I had passed more than one *mas* with a sign advertising *"Miel à vendre."* There would be a sweet ending to this American *maman's* outing—win or lose on the basketball court!

REFERENCES: *un cortège de mamans-au-volant* (m) = a procession of moms behind the wheel; *à la queue leu leu* = one behind the other; *le mouton* (m) = sheep; *la chaussette* (f) = sock; *un basketteur (une basketteuse)* = basketball player; *un clignotant* (m) = directional signal; *un mas* (m) = house or farm in Provence; *le miel à vendre* (m) = honey for sale

Also

cortège de = procession of
cortège nuptial = bridal procession
cortège funèbre = funeral procession

Décontracté
(day-kohn-trak-tay)

relaxed

$\mathcal{M}$y French family came for lunch yesterday. As usual, they brought the food, giving true meaning to the title of Hemingway's novel *A Movable Feast*. My husband and I were responsible for lawn mowing and *tables 'n' chaises* accessorizing. We assembled three four-legged surfaces and a funky chorus of chairs including lawn, antique Provençal, and could-fall-apart-you-bought-it-so-cheap. Three odd *nappes* covered any tabletop blemishes—*et voilà!*—we were ready to welcome the *belle-famille*.

Twenty in-laws arrived in four cars. Aunts, uncles, cousins, the *belle-mère* and the *beau-frère* spilled out, arms curved around gigantic *marmites* or flattened beneath fruit tarts.

The first time I met Jean-Marc's family, I was a jumble of nerves with wine flowing through my veins, which I tried to calm with enough Châteauneuf-du-Pape to sink a ship of drunken *matelots*. After that feat I zigzagged out of the *jardin*, stopping to slur *"Swaar!"*—g'night, y'all—before passing out in my future

aunt's *grenier.* She didn't mention it the next morning over croissants, though her lips seemed a little more pursed than I'd remembered them.

This time I was so relaxed that I could have melted onto my
cousin's layered chocolate cake, barely remembering what it felt
like during those first few years of adjustment, when all I seemed
to do was bump into walls. Sometimes I wonder if those walls
were brick-layered by *moi-même,* until I realize that, had I to do it
all over again, I'd bump my nose into each and every newly plas-
tered barrier just the same. Some trials scream to be lived
through, and a country's charm and beauty are no guarantee of
an easier, more seamless integration.

These days I savor the fruits of my labor as I fuss over my
French cousin, poke fun at my mother-in-law, or tell my *beau-
frère* that he'll have to wait for a second cup—that I'll be damned
if I'm going to serve one more café after laboring to get my cof-
feemaker to spit out twenty dainty cups of the stuff. It's my turn
to put my feet up and sip a little *sock juice.*

"There's no more toilet paper," a guest says.

"Oh—well—didn't you see the roll of paper towels?" I point
out. I had taken the trouble to break off a dozen perforated
sheets from the *rouleau,* ripping them neatly in half, before laying
them atop the roll, as any thoughtful hostess sans toilet paper
would.

When the *belle-famille* said their *au revoirs,* one of my littlest
cousins, eight-year-old Clara, said, *"Je ne veux pas partir!"* I know
what she means. I don't want to leave anymore either.

REFERENCES: *la chaise* (f) = chair; *la belle-famille* (f) = in-laws; *le beau frère* (m) = brother-in-law; *la marmite* (f) = cooking pot; *le matelot* (m) = sailor; *le jardin* (m) = yard; *swaar* (that is, *soir*) = g'night; *le grenier* (m) = attic; *moi-même* = myself; sock juice = coffee (the French refer to American—weak—coffee as *jus de chaussette*); *le rouleau* (m) = roll; *un au revoir* (m) = good-bye

Dédicace

(day-dee-kass)

noun, feminine

dedication

Sunday morning I woke up in the town of Agay. I looked out the barred window of our vacation rental and saw that the sea was calm. A rose-colored morning glow covered the sailboats in the bay, and the shutter on the fisherman's cottage was open; lace curtains were tucked behind the window's ears.

I put on my walking shoes and tiptoed out of the one-room bungalow. I walked past the *phare,* first stopping to read the plaque with its *dédicace* to the beloved French pilot and writer Antoine de Saint-Exupéry. I strolled along the boardwalk to a beach called Robinson Crusoe and paused at a villa with harmonica music seeping through a wall of tumbling geraniums; the red-white-and-pink flowers invited a few hungry bees to a sweet morning feast. I continued my *balade* past the lone fisherman, standing knee-deep in the sea. When I'd walked for twenty or so minutes, I did an impromptu turn on the heel and retraced my steps back to the sleepy bungalow. Quietly pushing open the door, I discovered my *petite famille* in attendance.

"*Salut, maman.*"

"*Bonjour, chérie.*"

The children and Jean-Marc had cat-ate-the-mouse expressions on their faces. Before I could say, "*Qu'est-ce qui se passe?*"—what's going on?—the tallest member of the trio invited me to sit down.

Next, Jackie presented me with a handmade greeting card that included a *poignée* of lavender (newly picked from the garden in front of our rented bungalow). Jean-Marc had strung the purple flowers through one of my business *cartes*. I turned over the card and read this message: "*Bonne Fête à la meilleure des mamans. Nous sommes tellement chanceux de t'avoir. Jean-Marc. Jackie. Max.*"

Next, Max sauntered into the room, cleared his throat, and recited the following text:

Bonne Fête à toi, ma maman.
Happy Mother's Day to you, my mom.
De tout cœur et très tendrement,
With all my heart and very tenderly,
Bonne Fête à toi, ma maman.
Happy Mother's Day to you, my mom.
Tant que tu me tiens par la main,
For as long as you hold my hand,
Je sais que tous mes lendemains

I know that all of my tomorrows
Sont pleins d'amour, de caresses,
Are full of love and caresses,
Et si parfois je te blesse,
And if at times I hurt you,
Si je suis désobéissant,
If I am disobedient,
Menteur, paresseux ou méchant,
A liar, lazy, or mean,
Si je prends plus que je te donne,
If I take more than I give,
Je sais que tu me pardonnes.
I know that you forgive me.
Aussi, je redis tendrement:
Therefore, I'll tell you again, tenderly:
Bonne Fête à toi, ma maman.
Happy Mother's Day to you, my mom.
———Jeanine Cougnenc

When silence filled the room, but for the gushing *va-et-vient* of the sea, the *maman* in question gathered the pajama-clad messengers into her arms and showered them with saltwater thanks.

REFERENCES: *le phare* (m) = lighthouse; *la dédicace* (f) = dedication, inscription; *la balade* (f) = stroll, walk; *la famille* (f) = family; *bonjour, chérie* (f) = hi, darling; *une poignée* (f) = handful; *la carte* (f) = card; *Bonne Fête à la meilleure . . .* = Happy Mother's Day to the best of moms. We are so lucky to have you; *le va-et-vient* (m) = comings and goings

Déguster
(day-goo-stay)

to savor

*F*or Jean-Marc's thirty-eighth birthday we dined at *Le Logis du Guetteur*, the castle-cum-restaurant at the top of our medieval village.

While the kids scooted off to discover the *lieux*, returning now and then smelling sweeter than before (had they been out to the garden to roll in the flowering rosemary?), Jean-Marc and I studied the menu.

"Thank God for Europe," Jean-Marc said, and we hushed a moment to listen to the various languages echoing in the stone-vaulted dining room: German, Norwegian, English. . . . Without the foreign tongues and the euros they generate, we would not be seated at this very table and so we gave a nod to tourism before unraveling the napkins and reaching for a just-baked roll.

I watch Jean-Marc swirl the salmon-colored wine in a gigantic glass.

"It's too dark," our friend the *sommelier* says, and shrugs.

"No, it's very good," Jean-Marc reassures him. True, rosé wine should be light, not too colorful, but there are exceptions to the rule, as my French teachers used to say.

The kids return from another jaunt around the hotel/restaurant—this time they smell like roses. . . . A visit to the *petit coin* solves the mystery. I notice the tall quarter-full *flacons* of free perfume in the bathroom, and realize my kids have splashed it on with abandon. I return to the table to tell them to remain seated, focusing my energy on their manners and keeping every crumb in place.

Jean-Marc offers his wineglass to a very coiffed and non-creased Max, who lifts his nose to the rim, inhales, and says, *"Pomme!"*

"Exact," his father replies.

The glass is passed to seven-year-old Jackie, whose nose hovers above the surface.

"Pêche!" she says.

"Tu as raison," Jean-Marc replies.

Each child has taken a small sip of wine after carefully swirling the contents in the glass and sniffing.

When the children are served *foie gras,* they reach for their bread.

"Regardez, les enfants." Look.

Jean-Marc cuts a small wedge from the dense *carré,* then puts the tip of the knife into his mouth, letting the *foie gras* melt atop his tongue. *C'est dommage* to put *foie gras* on bread, as if it were bologna.

While Max, Jackie, and Jean-Marc enlivened their taste buds

67

and gave the olfactory nerves something to shout about, I took in the scene before me: a French father handing down a gastronomic heritage to his children with the ease and lightness of a swirl in a glass.

Though I had not tasted the wine or the *foie gras,* my eyes were *en train de déguster*—savoring a morsel of life, a sip of so many isolated seconds forming one scrumptious scene. One sweeter than peaches, far from tart. Now a blink of the eye and swish, gulp, ahhh. More than a fleeting aftertaste, a souvenir for a lifetime.

REFERENCES: *le logis du guetteur* = the watchman's dwelling; *les lieux* (m, pl) = premises; *le sommelier (la sommelière)* = wine steward; *le petit coin* (m) = bathroom, powder room; *le flacon* (m) = bottle; *la pomme* (f) = apple; *exact* = correct, exact; *la pêche* (f) = peach; *tu as raison* = you're right; *le foie gras* (m) = pâté made from goose liver; *regardez, les enfants* = look, children (look, you guys); *le carré* (m) = square; *c'est dommage* = it's a shame; *en train de déguster* = in the process of tasting

68

Dent

(dahn)

noun, feminine

tooth

The Tooth Fairy *n'existe pas*! In France it is *La Petite Souris* who tucks a euro or two beneath a toothless child's pillow. . . .

At the dinner table, I struggle to get two kids to eat *haricots verts* with their *surimi* (the latter, a breeze). As Jackie forks green beans *à la crème* into her mouth with the enthusiasm of a French postal worker and the *vitesse* of a, well, French postal worker, I eye Max to make sure he's in rhythm with his table mates.

"I sure hope La Petite Souris will pass tonight," he announces with a wink and a toothless grin. I suddenly remember the front lower canine he gifted me with earlier.

"Yah, yah, just eat and *tais-toi*, all right!" I say, not wanting his sister to pose too many questions, which might lead to demythicizing the fairy/*souris*. Max was a seasoned pro at the tooth exchange, but it was still new and exciting to his sister.

"I'd be happy to get two euros," Max hints.

His request sends me back thirty years to when I, too, waited for *la fée*, who brought me twenty-five American cents a *dent*.

I remembered the insider information that Max gave his sister when it was her first time to be visited by La Souris. I was seated beside them folding laundry, separating *chaussettes*, *culottes*, and *gants de toilette* into neat piles when I overheard the following conversation:

"Five euros for a good *dent*, ten for a real white one."

"J'ai envie de dix," Jackie said, referring to the ten euros she hoped to find under her pillow the next morning.

"I don't know, Jackie, this one looks a little yellow. You'll probably get five for it *unless* La Petite Souris decides to give you a gift, in which case you may get seven euros."

My six-year-old collected her tooth, shutting it safely into the ring box she'd fished out of my closet.

I heard her up early that morning, counting, *"Un, deux, trois, quatre, cinq. Cinq euros."*

She pushed open the door to my bedroom and climbed up onto my bed.

"Do you have lots of money now, sweetie?" I had asked.

"J'ai trois sous," she replied, referring to the two two-euro coins and the one-euro coin in her hand.

I kicked myself for forgetting to let La Petite Souris in on Max and Jackie's "How much for a tooth?" conversation, but *he* had been watching a soccer match and by the time he carefully placed the coins under Jackie's pillow I'd already fallen asleep.

Daylight streamed past the *fenêtre* and I had pulled my

daughter close, trying to experience some of the magic, post-Souris. A metallic scent surfaced as she shuffled the coins in her hands, staring at them, not really understanding their worth.

"Maybe it's enough to buy a *bonbon*?" she said.

REFERENCES: *n'existe pas* = doesn't exist; *La Petite Souris* (f) = the Little Mouse (= the Tooth Fairy); *un haricot vert* (m) = green bean; *le surimi* (m) = imitation crabmeat; *à la crème* = with cream; *la vitesse* (f) = speed; *tais-toi* = be quiet; *la fée* (f) *(la fée des dents)* = fairy (the Tooth Fairy); *une chaussette* (f) = sock; *une culotte* (f) = underwear; *un gant de toilette* (m) = washcloth; *j'ai envie de dix* = I would like ten; *Un, deux, trois, quatre, cinq. Cinq euros* = One, two, three, four, five. Five euros; *j'ai trois sous* = I have three coins; *la fenêtre* (f) = window

71

Also

la dent de lait/de sagesse = baby tooth/wisdom tooth

Expressions

avoir les dents longues = to have long teeth, to be ambitious

donner un coup de dent à = to bite into

percer ses dents = to teethe

manger du bout des dents = to eat by the end of one's teeth, to pick at one's food

Dinde

(dand)

noun, feminine

turkey

*J*ean-Marc put in an order for the five-kilo turkey, then drove to the next village to pick it up. He had already telephoned his *maman* for her stuffing recipe, which calls for *morilles, foie de volaille, marrons, jambon cru, cèpes, gésiers,* and cognac.

My husband is always so *décontracté* about receiving guests and cooking for the masses. I don't know why that surprises me still. Here is a Frenchman who planned his entire wedding, inviting 150 people to share the happy day. (He would have invited five hundred if he had the *fric* to do so.)

The former *célibataire* called the priest, reserved the reception room, hired a DJ, composed the menu, selected the wines, ordered the flowers, printed the announcements, found lodging for my family, purchased the rings *and* had them inscribed inside, all while handling the complicated paperwork involved in marrying a blushing foreign bride. All I had to do was choose the *robe de mariée* and show up for the *essayage*. I am certain Jean-Marc would have lost the three kilos for me and stood in for the gown fitting if I had asked. That is just how enthusiastic and devoted he was—and ten years later, still is—to our union.

So—*évidemment*—I am mistaken to question whether or not such a man is capable of dressing a turkey. I was touched at Jean-Marc's suggestion that we celebrate Thanksgiving, and invite a group of French friends to join us, but when he said he was going to prepare the *dinde* I wondered if he was aware of how difficult it is to dress such a bird and get it cooked right. Not that I had the slightest idea how to do it. I just had heard it was hard and believed the rumors.

Mon mari would just have to discover that himself, I reasoned, as I left him to *plumer* the bird and headed to the backyard to hang out the laundry. By the time I returned to the kitchen, *la dinde avait disparu*.

"Where is the turkey?"

"In the *four*."

I looked over to the oven, where the bird was already taking on a golden hue.

C'est une farce! I thought to myself, looking around the kitchen, which was *nee-kel*.

"*C'est la farce de ma mère*," Jean-Marc said, smiling, handing me his mom's letter, the one with the stuffing recipe, to file.

I stopped a moment and looked the cook in the eyes. The reflection carried me back a decade, to the French Alps and a quiet path along a river, where a man and a woman stood in silence,

73

eyes locked in translation, until the man's unspoken thoughts were understood: "Everything is going to work out, trust me." Back in the kitchen, I blinked, having remembered again all of the reasons that led me to trust and to say "I do."

REFERENCES: *la morille* (f) = morel (mushroom); *le foie* (m) *de volaille* = poultry liver; *le marron* (m) = chestnut; *le jambon cru* (m) = raw ham; *un cèpe* (m) = cepe (mushroom); *un gésier* (m) = gizzard; *le fric* (m) = cash; *le célibataire* (m) = bachelor; *la robe de mariée* (f) = bridal gown; *un essayage* (m) = trying on, fitting; *évidemment* = obviously; *le mari* (m) husband; *plumer* = to pluck; *la dinde avait disparu (disparaître)* = the turkey had disappeared; *le four* (m) = oven; *c'est une farce* = it's a joke; *nee-kel* (for "nickel") = spotless, spic-and-span; *c'est la farce de ma mère* = it's my mother's stuffing

❧

Expressions

plumer la dinde = to rip someone off
être le dindon de la farce = to be the turkey of the stuffing, to be the victim, the dupe, of something or
someone

Dissemblance

(dee-som-blance)

noun, feminine

dissimilarity

From here to there, and from the Var to the Valley.
  From Provence to Paradise Valley.
  From parasol pines to palos verdes.
  From the mistral to the monsoon.
  From Smart cars to Suburbans.
  From quiche to quesadilla.
  From tarte to taco.
  From *bisous* to bear hugs.
  From baguette to bagel.
  From a *billet* to a buck.
  From *sanglier* to serpent.
  From the Mediterranean Sea to the Mojave Desert.
  From *service compris* to gratuity.

From couture to cowboy.
From *pays adopté* to homeland far away.

REFERENCES: *un bisou* (m) = kiss; *un billet* = bill (banknote); *un sangli-er* (m) = wild boar; *le service* (m) *compris* = tip included; *le pays adopté* = (m) adopted country

Douche

(doosh)

noun, feminine

shower

$\mathcal{A}$t the end of Marseilles, in the *petit port* of Callelongue, where limestone cliffs tower above a navy blue sea and charming *pointus* bob up and down in a postcard-perfect image, we spend a relaxing *après-midi*. A weatherworn fisherman sits atop a bucket, shelling prickly plum-colored *oursins;* he occasionally looks up to gawk at the *monde* that passes before him, including divers, hikers, and families out for a Sunday drive.

Callelongue is an old fishing village where families still inhabit, if only for a weekend, the *cabanons* their ancestors once called home. Some of the old shacks have been given a new front door and a new coat of paint. A sign on one *porte* reads *"Souvenir d'Enfance."* A childhood memory.

My *belle-mère* and I are perched over our plates, enjoying *le déjeuner.* She is eating *supions* and I am sharing the day's catch *(loup)* with Jean-Marc. Though we are eating fish, birds are on my mind.

Because of a recent catastrophic hotel accommodation I ask my *belle-mère:* "Do the French say '*bain d'oiseau*'?"

Michèle-France takes a moment to *réfléchir.*

"In English we say 'birdbath,'" I add.

"No, we don't say that here," she answers.

"Do you have an expression for when someone bathes from the sink? I mean, when there isn't a shower available?"

With that, my mother-in-law looks out to sea. . . . "Not long ago in France," she begins.

I learn about how the French used to fill porcelain bowls with water from a *pichet* in order to wash up. I am surprised that the French, who seem to have a delightful string of words to capture every idea, do not have a word for this, an equivalent for "bird-bath."

"You know," she confides, "the French have a *mauvaise réputation* for not bathing."

The confession colors my cheeks *rouge-tomate.* As I sit willing an innocent look on my face, an "Imagine that!" expression of surprise, my *belle-mère* leans in to the table and whispers, "Especially the Lyonnais! They are the smelliest!"

So as not to ruffle any French feathers (particularly if you happen to be from Lyons) and lest you think that the French really think that bathing is indeed for the birds . . . keep in mind that my *belle-mère, elle rigole!* And besides, *elle est Lyonnaise.*

REFERENCES: *le petit port* (m) = small port; *le pointu* (m) = small fishing boat; *un après-midi* (m) = afternoon; *un oursin* (m) = sea urchin; *le monde* (m) = world; *le déjeuner* (m) = lunch; *le supion* (m) = calamari; *le loup* (m) = sea bass; *un bain d'oiseau* (m) = birdbath; *réfléchir* = to think, to reflect; *un pichet* (m) = jug; *une mauvaise réputation* (f) = bad reputation; *rouge-tomate* = tomato red; *Lyonnais(e)* = someone from Lyons; *elle rigole (rigoler)* = she laughs, she jokes; *elle est Lyonnaise* = she is from Lyons

Also

les douches = shower room(s)

Expressions

une douche froide = a letdown, a terrible disappointment

prendre une douche = to take a shower

passer à la douche = to go for a shower

prendre une bonne douche = to get soaked

une douche écossaise = an alternately hot and cold shower

Égard

(ay-gar)

noun, masculine

consideration

After dropping Max off at *le basket,* Jackie and I entered the *boulangerie.* I waited in line, careful to guard *ma place* when the lady who walked in after me began inching forward. I've learned to stand my ground *chez la boulangerie, la poste,* and other public places where line cutters threaten to usurp one's spot.

Meanwhile a man walked in and announced, *"Bonjour, messieurs. Bonjour, mesdames,"* a typical greeting in France, and a polite thing to do when one enters a public *lieu.* I answered, *"Bonjour, monsieur,"* happy to fit in when and where I can.

I soon forgot about the *monsieur* and remembered to concentrate on the lady who had inched forward again.

Eventually I purchased my baguette and turned to leave, but was stopped by Monsieur.

"Could I have a word with you?" he began. "Each time I come

into a place I say *'Bonjour'* and no one responds. Thank you for responding."

I was moved and didn't know how to react. Walking back to my car I thought, No, thank you, monsieur, for showing me that even the French feel like a fish out of water sometimes.

REFERENCES: *le basket* (m) = basketball; *la poste* (f) = post office; *le lieu* (m) = place

Expressions

être plein d'égards pour quelqu'un = to be very consider-
ate toward somebody
manquer d'égards envers quelqu'un = to be inconsiderate
toward someone
avoir égards à quelque chose = to take something into
account
à bien des égards = in many respects

Élève

(ay-lev)

noun, masculine/feminine

student

Since landing in France twelve years ago, this *américaine* has been routinely approached by French parents seeking English lessons for their children. For some reason, the idea of a cash exchange between friends after tutoring always embarrassed me. I am more motivated now as I further a *qualité de vie*—a process that includes veering away from the Day Job in order to work more creatively from home.

So now Antoine arrives each Saturday morning at nine sharp. He pulls a pencil case from his *sac-à-dos* and begins the mania of arranging his writing utensils neatly across the desk. I'm forever amused by French pupils and their school supplies. Each and every *élève* has a variety of pens, pencils, erasers, correction fluid, rulers, and more, all crammed into a required *trousse*.

I am careful not to cause Antoine to mark down an error, having witnessed the time it takes to rectify the *faute*. A written mistake involves setting down his pen, selecting a liquid correcting instrument, effacing the error, and carefully returning the corrector pen to its place in line before penning in the correct letter. Although Antoine is extremely adept at this process, such corrections are time sensitive nonetheless.

Like every French student, Antoine keeps a detailed assignment book, or *mémorandum personnel*. At the front of the book, there is a page marked *"Emploi du Temps,"* and another for his *planning scolaire*. After those pages, the book becomes a calendar of the school year, one in which to note homework assignments and reminders of upcoming exams. The shuffle involved in checking teacher's instructions from his *mémorandum*, consulting the grammar book, then the exercise book . . . now over to the grid-lined *cahier*—that is another story entirely!

I want to tell Antoine to put aside his pens, paper, and persnickety ways if only for an hour; to sit back and listen, repeat, relax; to *tchatcher* with me for a "little hour"—the understanding will come, and no thanks to all that writing paraphernalia.

Instead, a vision of a nineteen-year-old woman comes to mind, one who had been given a second chance at an education after nearly failing high school. I thought about the insecure and fretful *étudiante* of French, and how her love for the subject caused her to begin turning her learning ways around, with rigorous study hours, meticulous notes—elaborated and "made clear" with the help of highlighters, multicolored pens, rulers, erasers, and Wite-Out; how she organized her notes into so many folders and three-ring binders, or with the help of staples, rubber bands, and paper clips, and recorded the class lectures, playing them back as she fell to sleep, hoping the unconscious mind would automatically seize all of the information and spit it out on the next day's exam. Remembering my own quirky, punctilious *apprentissage* of a foreign language, I realized with a smile of recognition that I'd once had my own overstuffed *trousse* and *planning scolaire*.

REFERENCES: *la qualité de vie* (f) = quality of life; *le sac-à-dos* (m) = backpack; *la trousse* (f) = pencil case; *une faute* (f) = mistake; *un emploi du temps* (m) = timetable; *un cahier* (m) = notebook; *tchatcher* = to chat; *un étudiant (une étudiante)* = student; *l'apprentissage* (m) = learning

84 • • • • • • • • • • • •  • • • • • • • • • • • •

Also

un/une élève professeur = student-teacher
un/une élève officier = officer-cadet

• •

Empoignade

(ahn-pwan-yahd)

noun, feminine

fight

We exited the *supermarché* and began to cross the first lane of the parking lot, Max in the lead, then me with the *caddie*, then Jackie. The white Peugeot 206 sped round the bend and I pivoted to reach for Jackie, backing up two feet to slow the oncoming car and glare into the window as I grasped for my six-year-old's hand. The car all but burnt rubber the second Jackie made it over the lane, its driver hardly patient for my daughter to pass. I grabbed the children's arms and hurried across two rows of parked cars to confront the offender, who had rounded another bend to park, unknowingly, opposite my car.

"Get in the car!" I said to the kids.

I stood glaring at the passenger, a man, who had gotten out of the white car. I was waiting for the driver, a woman, to get out.

She was taking her time; perhaps she sensed the impending *empoignade*.

"What's the matter?" the guy said.

"What is the matter with you?" I replied.

The woman finally got out, sneered my way, and I noted her resemblance to the French actress Béatrice Dalle; a twenty-something, more villainous Dalle. Another guy got out, and then they were three. . . .

The three hooligans mumbled insults among themselves.

"*Connards!*" I mumbled back.

"What's that?" one of the guys said.

"*Et les enfants!*"—and the kids! I said.

"In France, we use the crosswalk!"

Ha! I thought, and then realized that he already had me pegged for the foreigner that I am.

The foreigner that I am was finding it hard to spew out a biting retort.

The trio turned their backs and slunk toward the *supermarché*. My French life flashed before me. The injustice of a stranger's assuming comment—that I was the one being disrespectful—stung. Twelve years in France, "doing as the French," and all my efforts temporarily nullified in one instant.

I got into my car. On the third try I got the key into the ignition. I looked down to find my arms and legs shaking. While I waited for my nerves to calm, I turned to have a word with the kids.

"Did I embarrass you guys?"

"*Non, maman,*" said Max. Jackie agreed.

"Should I have said nothing?"

"Well, if you didn't say anything, they wouldn't have said any-thing back." I couldn't argue with Max.

Out of the mouth of French babes: wisdom and truth. And a reminder that it is futile to try to talk sense into hooligans: men, women, French, American, Dalle-faced or otherwise.

REFERENCES: *le caddie* (m) = cart; *un connard* (m) = idiot

87

Enfance

(on-fonce)

noun, feminine

childhood

$\mathcal{M}$ax celebrated his *neuvième anniversaire* on Monday.

"I don't feel nine," he said. "I feel like I'm seven years old!"

It took me a moment to understand his comment, but what he meant was, he feels great! (Well, apart from suffering a *mal de tête* most of the afternoon.)

My aunt and uncle from San Francisco called to wish Max happy birthday.

"I have a head cake," he explained, holding his head and struggling to find his English over the phone. I sat beside my son, whispering the correct words as I always do when the kids speak to their American relatives. "It's head*ache,* Max." My heart swelled as I smiled his way, encouraging him to continue to express himself in the foreign tongue that is his mother's native language.

Nine! I can't help but compare how different his life is from mine at that age. . . .

When I was nine, I lived in Aspen, not because we were rich—we were not—but because my mom was mending a broken heart. Her boyfriend had sent her, my sister, and me to Colorado, to get over him.

We lived in a two-bedroom apartment on the third floor. My mom sold ski apparel at Aspen Sports. I sold newspapers at a quarter a pop and spent my income on stuffed animals.

Max lives in a five-room villa in a medieval French village. His father sells Mediterranean wine. Max sells *tombola* tickets and has a savings account.

At nine I spoke fluent English and pig Latin. Max speaks fluent English and French.

I skied on weekends and stayed after school to be tutored in math. Max plays basketball and tutors his sister in *mathématiques.*

My favorite color then was green; his favorite is orange, pronounced *oh-ronzh.*

The grown-ups called me Squirt (I still don't know why) and my best friend was a boy named Chip. He was the fattest kid in fourth grade.

We call our son Mousse (short for Maximousse, which is not his real name either) and he doesn't have a *meilleur ami,* insisting he likes all his friends equally.

When I was nine, my favorite meal was my mom's soft corn tacos; if you ask Max what he wants for dinner he'll tell you, *"Œufs à la coque!"*

89

I wrote with my left hand. Max is a *droitier*. I still write with my left, and Max has taken to editing my writing with his right.

And although I don't remember having "head cakes" when I was nine, I did eat a fair amount of Twinkies.

REFERENCES: *le neuvième anniversaire* (m) = ninth birthday; *le mal de tête* (m) = headache; *une tombola* (f) = raffle; *un meilleur ami (une meilleure amie)* = best friend; *un œuf à la coque* (m) = soft-boiled egg; *un droitier (une droitière)* = right-handed person

Expressions

première enfance = infancy
l'enfance de l'art = child's play
la naïveté de l'enfance = the naïveté of childhood

Façon

(fa-sohn)

noun, feminine

way

I've lived in France long enough to walk oblivious past the lone sink in many a French bedroom. The cramped "toilets in a closet" no longer mystify me and the two-hour machine wash cycle is something I've come to organize my life around. But to outsiders, these *bizarreries* often bring puzzling looks. I sometimes wonder what my American guests are thinking when they come to camp *chez nous*. While our modern house—built in 1981—holds fewer curiosities, its Frenchness is hard to miss.

Here, when temperatures rise to 37 degrees Celsius, we condition the air by latching the heavy wooden shutters and closing double-paned windows so as to seal in any cool air collected during the early-morning hours.

When exiting the cramped, curtain-bare *douche,* our guests reach for a cardboard-stiff towel. Towels just about stand on their own after being burned dry beneath the *soleil de Provence,* and the upside is that there is no need for a space-usurping towel rack.

While some American homes have a basketball hoop, our place has a *boules* court. Out pitching heavy steel balls across a dusty yard, visitors must wonder just when dinner will be served, because back home in Arizona, the evening meal takes place somewhere between six and seven o'clock, not between eight and nine (or sometimes ten) as it does here.

Returning dinner dishes to the kitchen, my guests search the sink for that gurgling black void that has food disappearing with the click of a switch; noticing the permanent grid strainer instead, they turn to find the host scraping leftover bits of endive salad, potato *gratin,* and raspberry tart into the garbage can as is the custom in most French kitchens.

When it's time to hit the sack, overnighters may feel they have been sheet shorted, but it's really a matter of how some French families make up their beds: with the ever practical two-in-one *housse de couette,* or comforter cover, which eliminates the need for the *drap.*

"Well," say you, "your home is not so different from mine." Yes, but should you wake in the morning with a fever from having opened the shutters in the night (in your first attempt at French "air-conditioning"), would a stethoscope-toting Frenchman pay a house call that won't send you to the emergency room once you saw the bill?

92

REFERENCES: *les bizarreries* (f, pl) = oddities; 37°C = 98.6°F; *le soleil* (m) *de Provence* = sun of Provence; *les boules* (f, pl) (aka *pétanque*) = a traditional game played with heavy steel balls; *le gratin* (m) = casserole; *le drap* (m) = sheet

Expressions

de toute(s) façon(s) = at any rate, anyway
sans façon = unpretentiously
faire des façons = to make a fuss

Faute

(fowt)

noun, feminine

mistake

$\mathcal{S}$ince the age of five, when he went on his first school *sortie* to the baker's, Max has said that he wants to be a *boulanger* when he grows up. But I can tell you, as his *maman*, that his real talent lies in *rédaction*.

Many a night finds my son impatiently awaiting the rough draft of my piece for the next morning. While I brush my teeth, he is already shouting *"Faute!"* or *"Erreur!"* in the next room.

"Just a minute, let me finish brushing! And—I *know* there are *fautes*—it's what we call a rough draft, Max. Sheesh!" I tap my toothbrush five times against the sink, throw the *brosse à dents* into the enamel cup, and shuffle toward the editing chamber, aka my son's room.

For the next five minutes it's "We don't say this in French

and we don't say that." He's got my watermelon-colored ink pen, the one with the fake gold-flecked *encre,* and he's marking up the page. Well, maybe *he* doesn't say that—at least not yet, I remind myself before deleting the word or phrase in question.

In addition to correcting text, he has his opinions about readership, format, and style.

"Why don't you put the translation right after the word so people don't have to flip up and down the page? Besides, you'll save words—more money for you!" he says. I don't know how he has calculated this last point, but I am amused by his acumen.

I think over his suggestions, and am surprised by their value.

"You are nine years old! How do you know all this already?"

He raises shoulders to earlobes and flashes a new set of front teeth.

"You know, you would make a great editor," I say, at which point he reminds me of his baking aspirations. I selfishly hope he will be a *boulanger,* and live in the same village as me for life, and not some highfalutin editor who might get the bright idea to move to Paris or New York.

My son the *rédacteur* has been on me for months about my next book. "Is the cover ready? You know, the *couverture* is very important. It's best if you change a bit from the last one. You're not going to use the last one, are you?"

"Why don't I just put *your* picture on the cover?" I say. With that, he runs over to the bookcase, pulls one of his pictures from the shelf, and, pointing to the top of the photo, says "The title could go right here."

"Allez! Let me get back to work now."

"Don't forget about the cover," he says, pointing to his picture and winking.

REFERENCES: *la sortie* (f) = outing; *un boulanger (une boulangère)* = baker; *la rédaction* (f) = editing; *une erreur* (f) = mistake; *une brosse à dents* (f) = toothbrush; *l'encre* (f) = ink; *le rédacteur (la rédactrice)* = editor; *allez! (aller)* = go on! (get out of here!)

Expressions

une faute grave = gross misconduct

commettre une faute = to make a mistake

une faute de frappe = typo, typing error

une faute de grammaire = grammatical mistake

Fête Foraine

(feht fo-rehn)

noun, feminine

fair

Max and Jackie held their stomachs and gurgled with laughter. "*La fête farine!* She said '*la fête farine.*' Did you hear that, Jackie? Hahahahahaha!"

Once again my children were not laughing *avec moi* but *at* me. This time my gut-splitting gaffe was saying something that translated to "flour festival." I don't see what's so funny about that. Perhaps *fête farine* (I meant to say *fête foraine,* meaning a fair) is a leap from "carnival," but you might have a flour festival at a fair, *n'est-ce pas?*

"What I said was, if you don't calm down, I am not going to take you to *la fête FORAINE. Voilà!*"

The kids were *très sages* for the rest of the afternoon, and at 8 PM, accompanied by our friends from a neighboring *hameau,* we headed to the village *à pied.*

We chose a café far from the band and its blaring speakers, which meant we wouldn't be frequenting our favorite watering hole—*un peu délicat,* given that the owner is a friend of a friend. We hid behind our *paninis* at the neighboring café and were relieved to be able to hear one another speak.

"Bon appétit," the waiter said, and for a moment I worried about our sandwiches, which we had bought elsewhere, until I remembered that the French sometimes buy croissants and bring them to the café to have alongside their cafés au lait.

While the kids rode the scaled-down *manèges,* including the *autos tamponneuses* and the *chenille* (which shot out a *bonbon*-scented cloud) and ate *barbes à papa* and crêpes with Nutella, we talked about *tout et rien* and watched the villagers stroll by.

Having been raised in what is one of America's largest cities, I am forever charmed by the tiny village that I have called home for the past six years. It is so small that the whole fairground was set up along the narrow parking lot in front of the town hall, making parking a bit *compliqué* for a few days, though the townsfolk didn't seem to mind.

We watched the locals, who crowded around café tables under the star-spangled Mediterranean sky. There was the plumber eating a crêpe, the local drunk (who doubles as resident *mendiant*) clapping and chortling next to the bumper cars, and a slew of other Gallic characters.

And judging by the number of crêpe-toting carnie goers, you might have called it a flour *fête* after all.

REFERENCES: *la farine* (f) = flour; *avec moi* = with me; *très sage* = very well behaved; *un hameau* (m) = a hamlet (tiny village); *un peu délicat* = a little delicate; *le panini* (m) = grilled (Italian) sandwich; *bon appétit* = enjoy your meal; *un manège* (m) = fairground attraction, merry-go-round; *une auto tamponneuse* (f) = bumper car; *la chenille* (f) = caterpillar; *une barbe à papa* (f) = cotton candy (literally "papa's beard"); *compliqué* = complicated; *un mendiant (une mendiante)* = beggar

Also

les forains = fairground people, carnies
un spectacle forain = a traveling show

Feuille

(fuhy)

noun, feminine

leaf

It was swift. It was sudden. Fall rushed in seemingly overnight as is fall's *habitude* here in Provence.

While the obvious signs of *l'automne* are under way *(les feuilles mortes qui tombent)*, other events hint at fall's arrival. . . .

Such as when my husband says, *"Je vais faire un feu ce soir,"* or when we begin to use the *sèche-linge* instead of hanging the clothes out on the line.

I know fall is here when my husband begins to *tailler* the lavender into little round *boules* or when we have to move our little bunny rabbit César indoors.

It's fall when the school flyer circulates announcing class photos or when the famous *braderie d'automne* in Saint-Tropez begins.

Summer is over when those little funky hunting cars that

look like a cross between a Beetle and a *quatre-quatre* begin to file past our home, direction the *garrigue,* en route for the *chasse.*

Fall is here when my *belle-mère* is *fatiguée* and says, *"Ça doit être le changement de temps,"* or when not a *gosse* can be found in our yard at ten till seven at night.

And chilly fall has arrived when the café in town lists *Daube Provençale* as its *plat du jour,* instead of *Salade Niçoise.*

That is fall in our little neighborhood here in the eastern part of Provence. Perhaps it is not so different from fall *chez vous?*

REFERENCES: *une habitude* (f) = habit; *l'automne* (m) = autumn; *les feuilles mortes qui tombent* = dead leaves that fall; *je vais faire un feu ce soir* = I'm going to make a fire tonight; *le sèche-linge* (m) = clothes dryer; *tailler* = to cut; *la boule* (f) = ball; *la braderie* (f) *d'automne* = autumn clearance sale; *un quatre-quatre* (m) = four-wheel-drive vehicle; *la chasse* (f) = hunt; *fatigué(e)* = tired; *ça doit être le changement de temps* = it must be the change of seasons; *un(e) gosse* = kid; *la daube* (f) = meat stew, casserole; *le plat du jour* (m) = day's special; *chez vous* = in your area

101

Ficelle

(fee-sel)

noun, feminine

string, or stick of bread

C'est la Sibérie!" Marie-Françoise said, opening the door and ushering us in. Something terribly wrong happened to the charming wine-producing village of Châteauneuf-du-Pape since our last visit in September: the wind. Siberia indeed.

I pushed back my fake-fur-lined hood and traded a frozen cheek for a gloriously warm one: Jean-Marc's aunt kissed me twice. *"Entrez, entrez!"* she said.

Draping my parka over the *canapé* arm, I noticed how the *maison de village* had transformed since our last visit, when we, along with two dozen other sticky and exhausted grape pickers, sat around a makeshift table for the *repas de vendanges*. Then, the room was a dark, gray attic come to life by the jubilant souls of the pickers (and further brightened by a little *vin rouge*).

Now the walls were refinished, revealing an attractive rock pattern and creating a remarkable contrast to the modern ceiling beams. The crumbling wooden *poutres* had been replaced by iron. At the mezzanine's window, my breath caught at the spectacular sight of Mont Ventoux. Back inside the house, several levels down, the basement is affectionately referred to as Fort Knox and is where Jean-Marc's uncle keeps a personal gold mine of French wine.

We were in Châteauneuf-du-Pape for an evening and a day, in which Jean-Marc would be helping out his uncle with the bottling of last fall's grape harvest.

When Uncle Jean-Claude said, "Pass the *ficelle*," at breakfast the next day I automatically searched the table for a string. Instead I saw croissants, *pains aux chocolat,* and two scrawny baguettes. There was also *confiture* and spreadable butter, but no string.

"Pas de string," I said, and then I immediately realized he meant the "string thin" baguette. But it was too late. . . .

"No, I don't want *underwear!*" he teased, before pointing to the French stick baguette that had been right under my crimson cheeks.

Oh, *that ficelle.*

Grapes and wine (and cold wind!) are abundant in Châteauneuf-du-Pape, and so is my French family's warmth and sense of humor.

REFERENCES: *entrez, entrez! (entrer)* = come in, come in!; *le canapé* (m) = sofa; *la maison de village* (f) = village house; *le repas de vendanges* (m)

= harvest meal; *le vin rouge* (m) = red wine; *la poutre* (f) = beam; *la confiture* (f) = jam; *un string* (m) = underwear (the thong type)

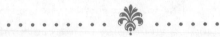

Expressions

c'est ficelle = it's not easy
tirer sur la ficelle = to exaggerate
tirer les ficelles = to pull the strings
voir la ficelle = to see how something is done
connaître les ficelles = to know the ropes
les ficelles du métier = the tricks of the trade
être mal ficelé = to be badly tied up (badly dressed)
déménager à la ficelle = to pack up and leave without paying

Fleuve

(fluv)

noun, masculine

river

Imagine a three-century-old bridge the color of mauve, its underbelly a mass of heavy stone slabs rising into a curve and becoming one in a line of arches across a shallow river. This is what Max, Jackie, Jean-Marc, and I can see from our canoe as we drift along, spending a lazy Bastille Day together.

Beneath the *pont* a Frenchwoman stands knee-deep in water, gently encouraging a few wide-eyed horses.

"Doucement," she says to them as we pass.

When we have floated past the hooves the three of us slide out of the *kan-oh-ay* and navigate, *à pied,* atop slippery rocks. The stream beneath the aqueduct is too shallow for the boat and we have to walk twenty or so meters before returning paddles to water.

Thousands of electric blue insects hover inches above the river Argens. *"Ce sont les demoiselles!"*—those are dragonflies!—

Max shouts from his rented kayak, which loops to and fro as he patiently awaits Jackie, Jean-Marc, and me in the slow-going canoe. My ten-year-old is enlightening us on the local flora and fauna. A *demoiselle,* we learn, is one of the two types of *libellules* that swarm along this refreshing sea-bound waterway. Max has already pointed out the *canetons* and turtles lest we'd missed them in our sluggish ride along the river.

A sheet of *nénuphars*—some flowering, most sleeping— covers parts of the *fleuve* and attracts clusters of royal blue *papillons.* Our shimmering path is flanked by *peupliers,* acacia, fig, and century-old chestnut trees. Thick groves of underwater branches sway beneath the river's mirroring surface.

Were you a bird high up in the *vidaubanais* sky, looking down, you'd witness paddles swatting to and fro in a chaotic attempt to advance. "Jackie! You are slowing us down," Jean-Marc shouts from the tail end of the boat.

"Oh! You're splashing me, Jackie. Careful with that paddle!" I say from the front.

And there, in the center of the canoe, one giggling seven-year-old girl is enjoying Bastille Day *à sa façon.*

REFERENCES: *le pont* (m) = bridge; *doucement* = easy does it; *kan-oh-ay* = pronunciation for *le canoë* (m) = canoe; *la demoiselle* (f) = young lady; *la libellule* (f) = dragonfly; *le caneton* (m) = duckling; *le nénuphar* (m) = water lily; *le papillon* (m) = butterfly; *le peuplier* (m) = poplar, aspen tree; *vidaubanais* = of Vidauban (small town in the Var region of France); *à sa façon* = in her own way

Expressions

un roman-fleuve = saga (novel)
un discours fleuve = lengthy speech

Fossé

(fos-say)

noun, masculine

ditch

I am one among those who hate to cut through other people's property—the kind of property that is unmarked *(sans mur)*, where there is a question as to whether or not the *terrain* is owned by anyone. I go to great lengths—*littéralement*—to avoid trespassing.

The other day, while out for a walk, I came to a fork in the road. Normally I'd walk left at the *fourchette*, where the official road continues, but on this particular day I paused to examine the narrow path to the right. Nothing unusual about this—I hesitate each time I arrive at the fork. And each time I go predictably, namby-pambily, left.

Cette fois-ci, I took a little step to the right—one small *pas*, then another—until I had one more step to go, at which point I looked left, then right. No one around. Who'd know, I thought, were I to commit a little *pied*-pushing peccadillo?

I'd seen the narrow path before, but never let my mind wrap around the possibility of setting foot upon it. My mom, when convalescing in France, had told me about "her" garden, located somewhere along that path.

"Mom, you can't just go hiking around the neighborhood and into people's gardens like that!" I warned. She just looked at me, with that roll-your-eyes expression that only she can accomplish while staring straight at you, pupils boring into pupils, unflinching.

"Well, if you ever want to join me, I'm usually in my garden late afternoon." With that, she turned on her heels and hiked off to her mysterious neck of the French woods.

"But it's not your gaaarrrrddeeeenn!" I shouted after her.

Garden. Pfft!! She was referring, I believed, to a plot of land, one in a row of dozens of village plots that is occasionally tended by a city slicker (read: a villager living one hundred feet away, in town).

My mom was not into keeping up appearances. Not anymore. Gone went the makeup, gone went the boots with spurs, gone went the *soutien-gorge*. Who needs a bra when she is *sans sein*? These nonessentials were replaced by one disarming smile and a new, if temporarily confined-to-this-village, wanderlust. Being treated for cancer had the effect of making her every day, her every hour, a new splendid discovery. Flowers now roared, the sky above electrified, each and every bird became a Technicolor version of its former self. My mom developed a new appreciation for people as she invited the whole village in. Into her *cœur*, that is. Tomorrow was for the *wet chickens* but today, today there was a garden, even if it didn't belong to her. "I have permission to use

109

it," she assured me, not that she answered to anyone anymore. (Not that she ever did.)

One day she got the idea to *meubler* her new grassy digs. She found the dilapidated lawn chair beside a garbage can in the village; the only *pépin* was how to get it to the garden, a one-hundred-foot vertical shuffle from the village. In the old days, she'd have lugged the chair up the hill herself, only now the muscles in her arms and legs had shrunk from so many hours spent bedridden.

Perhaps she sensed my disapproval; in any case she didn't ask me for help. Instead, she found two women from the village to lug that old chaise-longue up the hill. This was confirmed by my friend Alicia. "Oh, *that's* your mom," she said when we first met. "Yes, of course I know her. I dragged a lawn chair up the hill for her one day!"

Those are the memories and voices that flash and ramble through my head as I set one foot in front of the other, advancing along the Path Less Traveled. When I rounded the second bend, I found myself stepping into color, leaving the black-and-white immediate past behind. I had stumbled upon the *jardin. Her garden.* I was so excited to find it that I backed right into a ditch, and tumbled in.

The *fossé* was full of flowering weeds, which cushioned my fall. I crawled back out, dusted off my pant legs, and stood, in awe, before the garden. In the distance, I saw the village. The garden had a perfect *cabanon,* perfect not in condition but in charm. The rock shed was surrounded by a field of wild, colorful, can't-name-them-for-the-life-of-me flowers.

I pictured my mom there, on her lawn chair, iced-tea *en main,* glancing out over the village below. After a period of silence, the kind where you can't tell if several minutes have passed, or one whole hour, I raised my arm and a make-believe glass, and whispered, *"Santé!"* I told the lady with the hiking boots and concave chest that her garden is a real treasure. That I'm sorry it took me so long to come and visit, but that I will be back again soon. That maybe I'll drag my own lawn chair up next time, so as to see the view from her perspective.

REFERENCES: *sans mur* = without a wall; *le terrain* (m) = land; *littéralement* = literally; *cette fois-ci* = this time; *le pas* (m) = step; *le pied* (m) = foot; *le soutien-gorge* (m) = bra; *sans sein* = without a breast; *le cœur* (m) = heart; wet chicken = *la poule mouillée* = coward; *meubler* = to furnish; *le pépin* (m) = snag; *le jardin* (m) = garden; *en main* = in hand; *santé* = to your health! (cheers!)

Expressions

sauter le fossé = to make a risky decision
le fossé culturel = the cultural gap
le fossé entre les générations = the generation gap

Gaspiller

(gas-pee-yay)

to waste

$\mathcal{M}$y husband has taken to cooking like fluffy French bread to a plate of vinaigrette.

"J'aime cuisiner," he reports, as I watch a paper-thin crêpe do a backflip midair. He *is* good at crêpes, even if he does use the hand mixer to combine the ingredients. I promise not to say, "It's best to use a fork. The mixer will let in too much air." But I say it anyway—I can't help it.

"I like to do it this way," he says, catching the thin cake. "Ha!"

Yesterday's *plat du jour* included *le bar avec son printemps des légumes encore surgelés* (sea bass with frozen vegetables). Jean-Marc had put the whole fish—the head (with its shiny, unforgiving eyes), tail, and all—into a casserole dish before popping a square of frozen vegetables from box to dish. I returned to the oven's window time and again, to see just when the box form would melt down, level with the bass. The fish turned out well. The vegetables were chilly.

I never know what the children and I are going to eat when the call *"À table!"* goes out. One thing is sure: the *repas* will be colorful, its accompaniments motley.

My frugal French gourmet also saves everything. If it can fill a tablespoon, it is salvageable. *"Je le mangerai!"*—I'll eat it!—he insists. Open our fridge and you'll find all kinds of unlikely and still edible *rescapés:* a large plate with three little tortellini peering back, or a half piece of toast with olive spread. I've even found a half glass of water. (He does turn off the water when he soaps up in the shower, so why am I surprised?)

Every morning he puts Jackie's leftover bowl of cereal back into the fridge. I open the frigo midday to find the soggy floating puffs glaring back at me. *Beurk.*

At least he now covers leftovers in plastic wrap. It used to be I'd open the refrigerator door to find my mother-in-law's delicate chocolate cake naked against a bowl of Mediterranean mussels, still drunk, smelly, and a bit rude from the white wine sauce they were cooked in.

He has a few idiosyncrasies, in keeping with his "waste not" approach: like mixing the pasta du jour with yesterday's noodles. I'm not fond of the mélange of clunky macaroni pieces and fine angel hair pasta, and I don't like yesterday's red sauce mixed with today's Roquefort dressing.

His penchant for leftovers is witnessed in what accompanies most of his signature dishes: like scrambled eggs with four-day-old *poivrons grillés,* or mussels and a side timbale of last week's *soupe de cresson.*

"I thought that expired," I say, eyeing the shot glasses of soup.

"No, I just put it in the freezer."

"You put it in the freezer yesterday, after it sat in the fridge for a week?"

"Oui. So it wouldn't expire."

I go to great pains to throw out expired items, folding them under the other items in the garbage, deep into the can. Otherwise, *"J'ai trouvé ça"*—I found this—he'll say, recovering a decomposing *pomme de terre.*

"How'd that get there?" I'll say, dropping my jaw in a look of horror. Next thing I know, he's cut the bad parts out and tossed it in the pan for a soon-to-be *plat du jour. "Bon appétit!"* says he.

I can't say that the way to an American woman's heart is through her—in my case, weak—stomach, but enthusiasm for life (and for languishing potatoes) is downright irresistible in my cookbook.

114

REFERENCES: *j'aime cuisiner* = I love to cook; *à table!* = time to eat (everyone to the table!); *le repas* (m) meal; *un rescapé (une rescapée)* = survivor; *le poivron grillé* (m) = grilled pepper; *la soupe de cresson* (f) = watercress soup; *la pomme de terre* (f) = potato

Also

le gaspillage = waste

un gaspilleur/une gaspilleuse = a squanderer

Expressions

Quel gaspillage! = What a waste!
gaspiller son argent/son talent = to waste one's money/talent

. . . .

Glaçon
(glah-sohn)

noun, masculine

ice cube

$\mathcal{J}$ust when I think I have melded in with the scenery, there is something to trip up my blending in with the French. This happened again on Saturday as I sat at an outdoor café in Draguignan, the capital of the Var region.

On that gray-skied morning, a few inconsequentials became symbolic of my everlasting status as an *étrangère:* the single melting *glaçon* that arrived in the tall glass of *Coca Light* I ordered from the waitress, when ice cubes are optional, not assumed, in France, and the lingering American accent that I cannot seem to exorcise.

"C'est quoi ce temps?"—what's up with the weather?—I said to the waitress in my best French, eager for her to know me as one of her kind, that is, a local, sort of . . .

"Ah, for a tourist, it must be such a disappointment!" she replied, dashing my hopes yet again.

I shook the frozen cube in my glass, smiled into the cup in resignation, and answered: *"Oui, madame."*

REFERENCES: *un étranger (une étrangère)* = foreigner; *Coca Light* = Diet Coke

Gorgée

(gor-zhay)

noun, feminine

sip

The French island of Porquerolles is haunted in wintertime. The wind howls, taking on a silent scream as it whirls through the port to the sailboats, through the mastheads, coming out the other end in one eerie and constant moan. I listened to the cries of the *mistral* throughout the night from the safety of an over-heated hotel room.

"No, the island is not haunted," Jean-Marc assures me over breakfast the next morning.

"Well then, the locals are very strange!"

"That's due to interfamily marriages," he says, kidding me, as I continue to obsess about the idea that everything is somehow off, though I can't put my finger on just what.

"You could use some fresh air," he says, setting down his coffee. With our backs to the village, we set out to discover the island, with its fields of stark vines beneath the hilly *garrigue,* the latter shaded with an abundance of parasol pines that reminded me of giant broccoli. We advanced along the *sentier* in silent bliss, until our bodies warmed up and the heat began to get to us. That's when Jean-Marc asked: "Did you bring water?"

"No. And you?"

"Don't worry about it," Jean-Marc said. "If we see some people, we can ask for water."

We had two backpacks with food and fishing equipment, including Jean-Marc's homemade "mop spear," a rakelike contraption that he had fashioned from a mop and a fork in order to collect sea urchins. We were so prepared, with our store-bought salads, fresh bread, napkins, little packets of salt and pepper and yet—how could we have forgotten water! What would we wash lunch down with? Forget about lunch—how were we going to quench our thirst? My lips began to parch as we got farther and farther away from the hotel and from any possibility of obtaining fresh water.

I don't like asking for things, especially from strangers. And the idea of soliciting water, something so *intime*—as it would have to come from a stranger's flask and not a fountain—horrified me. I'd much rather make the forty-five-minute loop to the hotel and back to avoid asking for a *gorgée* from someone's *gourde.*

Perched at the end of a magnificent *falaise,* Jean-Marc located a populated cove and suggested we hike over to it and have our picnic *sans eau* there.

"I'm not thirsty," I said, guessing his plan.

"Don't worry. We won't ask for anything to drink!"

We reached the seashore and said *"Bonjour"* to the other hikers, who had a veritable wet bar of drinks at their feet: beer, Orangina, red wine, plain and sparkling water. Gulp.

Jean-Marc waded out to sea, braving the ice-cold waters, homemade spear in hand, and began hunting his beloved *oursins*. The fork part of his spear wasn't for stabbing, but for raking in the prickly sea urchins.

The four men on the picnic blanket ahead of ours became interested in the spectacle: beneath the sky of winter, a man waist-deep in chilly waters raking the floors of the sea with a curious fishing instrument.

Soon, their mouths began to water for the succulent *oursins*. I saw the men staring disappointedly into their picnic baskets— dry sandwiches made with ham tucked into day-old baguettes.

120

I watched my husband out at sea and noticed that his movements were a bit exaggerated. Retrieving an *oursin,* he would hold it up to the light like a rare gem, giving the beach gawkers an eyeful.

Three other hikers picnicked behind us; they also had dry ham sandwiches. Currently they chewed the ends of the baguettes, and from the look on their faces, they might as well have been chewing on the rubber sole of a shoe.

Meanwhile, there was my husband, raking in the violet sea urchins by the dozen from a now turquoise sea. I could almost taste the delicate orange mousse inside, and so, it appeared, could the gawkers.

That's when I realized what my clever husband was up to: the *troc.*

When he returned to shore with thirty or so sea urchins, the one fisherman, dry sandwich in hand, spoke:

"You didn't take the black ones, did you?"

"*Non.* The black ones are no good," my husband replied.

The fisherman peered into Jean-Marc's basket.

"Only the violet ones," Jean-Marc confirmed. "Mmm mmm . . ."

The French, particularly from this part of the *Hexagone,* have a soft spot in their hearts for sea urchins. You could probably trade a coveful of urchins for a veritable well of Evian water.

My husband's thoughts mirrored mine, and he scissored open the thin spiny animals, offering the prepared shells to the fishermen sans fish.

"Would you like some wine?" they asked, a bit embarrassed. Jean-Marc nodded and the men handed over the bottle when we couldn't provide a cup. Jean-Marc proceeded to swig with complete strangers.

I declined.

Next, my expert at barter and trade handed over a few more *oursins,* having carefully scissored them open to reveal a bright star design inside. Sea urchin roe is a delicacy. They say it takes ten fresh sea urchins to yield one half cup of roe. We sat on our blanket, spooning the roe from shell to mouth.

"Would you like some water?" the fisherman sans fish asked, raising a plastic bottle and eyeing the *oursins.* I studied the bottle, which was half full.

Jean-Marc looked at me hopefully.

My eyes pleaded back. What about spit?

Jean-Marc shook his head casually.

Spit . . . spit . . . spit, I thought.

It was then I noticed my husband's scraped hands as he sat there, the cracked, gutted *oursins* scattered about him. There was only one thing to do. Sip.

REFERENCES: *le sentier* (m) = path; *intime* = intimate; *la gourde* (f) = water bottle; *la falaise* (f) = cliff; *l'eau* (f) = water; *le troc* (m) = exchange; *l'Hexagone* (m) = France

Expression

boire quelque chose d'une gorgée = to drink something in one gulp

Goût

(goo)

noun, masculine

taste

Max volunteered his *maman* to assist on a field trip for the Semaine du Goût, or Taste Week, which was under way in France. The program was created to initiate French children into the pleasures of the palate and to give the would-be gastronomes a behind-the-scenes look at the method behind French baking madness.

The eve of the outing, Max gave me the lowdown on how to proceed: I was to park my car next to the *boules* court, enter the school yard with him and his sister, and proceed to class.

"Oh—and please don't wear your hair in a chignon!"

Needless to say, the next morning I took extra care grooming. Clearing the plates at the breakfast table, I announced that I was going to put on my makeup.

"Bonne idée!" Max said, with a little too much enthusiasm.

Keeping twenty-seven kids in line, or *en rang,* as we headed down the busy Boulevard Gambetta, past the train station to the CFA cooking school, was a small *épreuve.* The children stumbled on and off the *trottoir* like little drunken *matelots.*

Sur place, the kids were divided into two groups in order to participate in the *ateliers.* Half of the class went to the *atelier pâtisserie* to make chocolate cake, while the other half went to the *atelier boulangerie* to make bread.

While the *apprentis* helped the children measure chocolate into the *recipients,* I had a word with the *chef d'atelier:* "I heard the American brownie came into being as the result of one chef's failed chocolate cake," I said.

"Ah, bon?" he said, with a *méfiant* look on his face.

On second thought, I realized it probably was a bad idea to participate in shop talk with a pro, especially when I could not remember my sources for the brownie story, and so it was a great relief when the *chef* returned to the head of the class to resume instruction.

"Do you know where the word *goût* comes from?" he began.

My hand flew up, "Oh! Oh! Oh!" Did I ever . . .

A smile formed across Max's face, as if to say: she covered *that* item in her word journal yesterday.

REFERENCES: *la bonne idée* (f) = good idea; *en rang* = in line; CFA = *centre de formation d'apprentis* = apprentice training center; *une épreuve* (f) = an ordeal; *le trottoir* (m) = sidewalk; *le matelot* (m) = sailor; *sur place* = on the spot; *un atelier* (m) = workshop; *une pâtisserie* (f) = pastry; *un* apprenti (une apprentie) = apprentice; *un récipient* (m) = container; *ah, bon* = oh, really?; *méfiant(e)* = suspicious, distrustful

Expressions

sans goût = tasteless
de bon goût = in good taste
avoir du goût = to have good taste
à chacun son goût = to each his own
un goût passager = a passing fancy
prendre goût à quelque chose = to take a liking to something
le goût du terroir = the taste of the soil, food, or drink
  with a native tang

125

Gratter
(gra-tay)

to scratch

At Isa's house we sip aperitifs from colorful stemmed glasses and study the *pelouse*.

"We should have planted ours that way," Jean-Marc says. We had considered *les rouleaux de gazon*, or rolls of grass, but decided to scatter seeds instead. In spite of so much hard soil, the grains have pushed up green—just not all in one place. *"Grattez-les,"* the neighbor tells us, pointing to the dry patches. "Then replant."

Back at Isa's we are gathered on the tiled patio, still staring at the *gazon*. Manou hesitates. "I don't dare walk on it."

Isa, in a long black linen dress, puts her glass down, gathers the sides of her dress, and leaps out onto the *gazon*. She jumps up and down a half dozen times, stomping and giggling. "Don't worry! You can stand on it!" she says. Reassured, we move out to the grass, some of us taking our shoes off to feel the cool blades undertoe.

I am uncomfortable standing on French grass; all those

"*Respectez la Pelouse*" signs—atop even the smallest patch of grass in France—come back to haunt me, so that what we are doing feels illegal, even if our hostess has given us carte blanche to step there.

As if the grass weren't greener *chez* Isa, the view of the Rocher de Roquebrune is *for-mee-dah-bluh*. "It always reminds me of the Wild West," Barbara says. The famous red rock brings me back to my native Arizona, specifically to the majestic red buttes in Sedona.

The French continue to *tchatcher* and I wander over to where the lawn falls off like one of those never-ending swimming pools. Below, I see the Mediterranean forest, and beyond, the Rocher. I think that if Isa's grass were mine, I'd pull up a chaise longue, facing it to that red rock, and spend hours just staring at it while listening to the French birds sing as they are doing now. Then I think about how Isa probably can't pull up a chair often because she is so busy working outside the home and caring for two small children, and realize that I probably wouldn't be able to do so for those very same reasons.

Returning to the *tchatcheurs*, I decide that envying my friend's grass isn't going to make the green stuff miraculously push up *chez moi* and remember that the only way to have something you want is to *gratter* for it.

REFERENCES: *la pelouse* (f) = grass; *le gazon* (m) = grass or lawn; Manou = endearment for the name Emmanuelle; *for-mee-dah-bluh = formidable* = great; *gratter* for it (Franglais) = scrape (save) or work for it

Also

le gratte-ciel = skyscraper
le gratte-dos = back scratcher
le gratte-papier = pen pusher
le gratte-pieds = shoe scraper

Expressions

ça me gratte = it itches
gratter du pied = to be impatient
faire sa gratte = to make an illicit profit
gratter quelques francs = to earn a bit on the side
gratter les fonds de tiroir = to scrape the bottom of the barrel

Grignoter

(gree-nyo-tay)

to snack

At around a quarter to six the other night I had *un petit creux*. I knew it was a bit early to eat dinner, and the *goûter* hour had passed, so I felt a tinge of *mauvaise conscience* heading toward the *frigo*.

At the fridge I slid out a couple of plastic containers, pulling off the tops and emptying a few heaping tablespoonfuls of each salad onto a plate, drizzling my favorite olive oil over everything and cracking salt and pepper from the mill on top of that. I was making my way to the table when, unexpectedly, *la gêne* overcame me. I didn't want my French husband to see me eating at such an odd hour. The French don't eat in such a wayward fashion: it's breakfast, lunch, and dinner, with one clearly defined snack hour—and this wasn't 4 PM.! I made a U-turn back to the kitchen counter and huddled over my plate, managing to enjoy the leftovers from *Pâques* while standing.

If I'd been back home in my native Arizona, and if this were the day after Thanksgiving, I'd be seated comfortably in front of the television, eating platefuls of macaroni salad and turkey at any odd hour of the day. . . . I might even be washing the leftovers down with a Corona Light.

As it was, I was snacking on tabbouleh and *pois chiches,* and sipping a Diet Coke. My husband walked past, stopping briefly to notice me sidled up to the kitchen counter.

"Tu as une petite faim, chérie?" he asked, concerned, and seeing past my *cachette* as he always does.

This reaction is so French of him. I don't know what it is with *les Français,* and it certainly is in the spirit of politesse, but they must, simply *must* make a remark when someone is eating. Whether you are seated in the car at a stoplight munching on *pommes frites* or wolfing down a ham and cheese sandwich on a park bench, or nibbling on a croissant just outside the train station, complete strangers—passersby from all *niveaux sociaux* find it beyond their control not to stop and wish you *"Bon appétit!"*

My husband paused another moment before I looked up, cheeks bulging from *pois chiches,* face *rouge-tomate,* and nodding stupidly. I picked up my plate, walked back to the table, and sat down comfortably before the television, which I didn't bother to turn on.

REFERENCES: *un petit creux* (m) = a little hunger; *un goûter* (m) = snack; *une mauvaise conscience* (f) = guilty conscience; *la gêne* (f) = embarrassment; *Pâques* (m) = Easter; *un pois chiche* (m) = chickpea; *tu as une petite faim, chérie?* = are you a little hungry, darling?; *une cachette* (f) =

hiding place; *une pomme frite* (f) = a French fry; *le niveau social* (m) = social standing

Expressions

grignoter du terrain = to gain ground
grignoter entre les repas = to snack between meals

Gronder

(grohn-day)

to tell off, to scold

In 1993, Jean-Marc bought a small cottage perched in the hills of the Roucas Blanc, one of Marseilles's most charming neighborhoods.

The house, all of forty-five square meters, was divided into four tiny rooms, with the bathroom outside. Although there was no real *terrain*, there was a nice view of the Mediterranean Sea from the *terrasse*, as well as a stunning sight: the historic Notre-Dame de la Garde Basilica, just *en face*, which was lit up for a dramatic presentation each night.

Jean-Marc gutted the house into a studio and expanded the far wall all the way back to, and including, the ancient *mur* outside. Although this last detail was a bit illegal, it made for quite a cool conversation piece in our *salon*, and added two precious square meters to our cozy abode.

The wall expansion left us with one great dilemma: where to reroute the rain gutter. As the house was attached to another *maison* on the east side, there seemed no other option but to go west.

Jean-Marc figured that the drainpipe could empty into the neighbor's garden—a downpour of H_2O couldn't harm the begonias growing below. Though I felt uncomfortable with his reasoning, I had to admit the neighbor's flowers did look a bit thirsty and so I went along with the watering plan.

Returning from work one day, I pushed open the gate to our tiny patio garden. I was climbing the stairs to the front door when suddenly the neighbor's shutters burst open, and out came the elderly lady's torso *à la* jack-in-the-box. Next thing I knew, a barrage of complaints followed—a veritable *gronderie*. The woman's plastic hair curlers and bathrobe did nothing to diminish her fierceness, and I stood frozen, trying to decipher angry French. Soon enough the window slammed shut and I ran into the house, locking myself behind the door.

We eventually rerouted the drainpipe, and soon found ourselves invited once again to our neighbor's home, where we were treated to dainty lemon cakes, or madeleines, and herbal tea, followed by a less severe admonition to *faire gaffe* the next time.

133

REFERENCES: forty-five square meters is roughly 485 square feet; *la terrasse* (f) = balcony; *en face* = opposite; *le mur* (m) = wall; *le salon* (m) = living room; *la gronderie* (f) = scolding; *faire gaffe* = to be careful

Also

grondeur, grondeuse = grumbler, shrew

gronder contre quelqu'un = to grumble at someone, find fault with someone

gronder quelqu'un d'avoir fait quelque chose = to scold someone, to tell someone off, for having done something

Haleine

(al-ehn)

noun, feminine

breath

There are two things that cause bad breath."

My son is seated at the kitchen table explaining *la mauvaise haleine* to his little sister. I'm at the sink, sleeves rolled up and peeling potatoes, pausing only to heed Max's lesson on halitosis.

"Onions and Camembert," he informs her.

"Ah!" she says. "What is bad breath?"

"It's when somebody smells bad from the mouth."

With that he puts down his fork, leans toward his sister, drops his jaw, and exhales, "Haaaahhhhh."

This causes her to giggle. "Now you try," he says. "Go ahead, breathe out!"

Jackie leans forward, rolls her *noisette*-colored eyes to the sky, and pushes out her tongue with a dramatic "Haaaaahhhh."

Max's face contorts. His little freckled nose bunches up,

drawing with it his upper lip, exposing a row of new front teeth. A veritable grimace of *dégoût*.

"Your breath smells like Camembert. *Beurk!*"

"Haaaahhhh," Jackie repeats.

"Arrête, Jackie!"

"Haaaaahhhh."

"Ça suffit! Stop!"

Jackie is glowing from the discovery of yet one more way to *embêter* her brother. With this new torture information safely filed into her six-year-old brain, she rolls her eyes back level with mine and pulls in her tongue in time to say, *"Encore du Camembert, s'il te plaît!"*

REFERENCES: *noisette* = hazelnut; *le dégoût* (m) = disgust; *arrête (arrêter)* = stop; *ça suffit! (suffir)* = that's enough!; *embêter* = to annoy; *encore du Camembert, s'il te plaît!* = more Camembert, please!

Expressions

avoir mauvaise haleine = to have bad breath

tout d'une haleine = in the same breath

avoir l'haleine courte = to be short of breath or short-winded

perdre haleine = to lose one's breath

rire à perdre haleine = to laugh until one's sides ache

reprendre haleine = to catch one's breath

discuter à perdre haleine = to argue nonstop

retenir son haleine = to hold one's breath

un travail de longue haleine = a long and exacting task

d'une seule haleine = in the same breath (without inter-
    ruption)

tenir quelqu'un en haleine = to hold somebody spell-
    bound; to keep somebody in suspense

• •

137

Haricot Vert

(ah-ree-ko vehr)

noun, masculine

green bean

At the seaside town of Agay, just up the coast from Saint-Raphaël and along the *mer Méditerranée,* we rent a two-room bungalow, *à deux pas* from the sea.

Jackie and I prepare *haricots verts* for the *souper.* I hand my daughter a butter knife and a few pointers on how to prepare the green beans, and sooner than I can say *"Capeesh?"* she's begun.

Before long, I give up the knife, preferring to snap off each end of the bean. Jackie works her butter knife, carefully sawing off the pointy *haricot* ends. *"Comme ça?"* she says each time.

We sit tableside in swimsuits and flip-flops, chatting and chopping, pushing hair out of our faces with the backs of our arms, and watching the pile of beans diminish thanks to our sous-chef accord.

"Il est beau," she says, when the subject of Clément Dupuis comes up.

"What's more important, Jackie, a good-looking friend or a nice one?"

"*Beau et gentil,*" she replies.

Humph. I find it hard to argue with that, and switch subjects, promising her the astronomical sum of 2 euros 30 if she helps me finish the *haricot* task.

Considering the labor involved, I know it is a lot of money, but the *sous* will serve as a *bonbon* account for our two-day *séjour*.

Beau. Gentil. Bonbon. Haricots. Tchatching with a six-year-old on a lazy *après-midi*. Nothing could be finer.

REFERENCES: *la mer Méditerranée* (f) = Mediterranean Sea; *à deux pas (de)* = a few steps (from); *le souper* (m) = dinner; *capeesh?* (American slang for the Italian *capisci?*) = understand?; *comme ça* = like this; *il est beau* = he is handsome; *gentil (gentille)* = nice; *le sou* (m) = money; *le séjour* (m) = stay

139

Expressions

c'est la fin des haricots! = it's all over!

des haricots = nothing at all or a very small amount

courir sur le haricot = to run on someone's bean, to importune, to get on someone's nerves

Illico
(ee-lee-ko)

pronto

$\mathcal{I}$ was flipping through the pages of a popular French fashion magazine when my breath caught on an item midcolumn.

It wasn't another one of those risqué photos that had my eyes popping out of their sockets, or the *prix astronomique* of a runway model's *escarpins,* but a word. A fantastic word! A stylish, must-have *mot!*

Illico.

My lips trembled. I could not wait to pronounce the three-syllabled discovery. *Ee-lee-ko. Voilà!* Rushing back to the page to rediscover the new word, I found the writer tormenting fashion victims with thoughts such as "October is around the corner. You don't seriously plan on stretching that summer wardrobe *that* far, now do you?" The journalist then went on to explain fall fashions, which include panther prints, thick cinched-around-the-waist belts, fur, tartan, *cuissardes,* knee-length skirts, metallic fabrics, jodhpurs, and last but not least, the bolero!

Somewhere in that paragraph my text-roving eyes came to an abrupt halt with the word *illico*.

I immediately looked it up in the dictionary, willing it to be a French word. *Hélas,* no!

Illico is Italian. But the French use it, and that means that it is utterable now—*tout de suite*—*illico!* Just to be sure, I asked my French friend Barbara, who replied, *"Bien sûr! 'Illico presto,'* we say!"

My heart soared with the possibilities.

To the children I might now say, *"Allez. Au lit—illico presto!"* To bed now!

To the nice lady at the *poste: "Envoyez-le. Illico!"* Send it off. Right away!

To the neighbor's cat who is a constant menace to our little bunny, César: *"Allez! Va-t-en! Illico presto!"* Go on! Get out of here! Now!

I don't know if I'll be wearing tartan, panther, or *cuissardes* this fall. But when my tongue can find nothing else to throw on, there will always be *illico.*

REFERENCES: *un prix astronomique* (m) = astronomical price; *un escarpin* (m) = a pump (heel); *un mot* (m) = word; *les cuissardes* (f) = thigh boots; *hélas* = unfortunately

French synonyms for *illico: immédiatement, aussitôt, instantanément, sur-le-champ, sans délai, tout de suite, à l'instant, sur l'heure*

141

Expressions

illico presto = pronto (tout de suite)
partir illico = to leave at once

Imparfait

(am-par-fay)

imperfect

There is a verb tense in the French language known as the *imparfait*. It is used to describe past actions or states that were not completed. I have lived in France for more than a decade now, often feeling tense and incomplete when I compare myself to the French, in particular to the other women.

On a recent trip to the quaint village of Varage, in which my husband and I shared a country home with another couple and our respective children, once again I felt I was not living up to what I perceived were French high standards. During our week's stay I studied the Frenchwoman and noticed how she fussed over her children.

For lunch and dinner the French children have three- and sometimes four-course meals. A starched bib carefully tied around the child's neck, the feast begins. The main dish includes a garden vegetable (organic), a fresh catch such as trout, and a plate of local goat's cheese; after the cheese comes homemade yogurt *à la fraise.*

I prepare my children's meal: an all-in-one pork-chops'n'applesauce medley. While I scrape globs of applesauce off my daughter's T-shirt, the Frenchwoman scours the sink with bleach—her children are already out playing in the front yard.

At the swimming pool the Frenchwoman changes her children's wet bathing suits, replacing them with dry ones. My children see this and, having no change, take off their wet suits and run naked around the pool, their crimson-faced mother looking on.

I relax back into my lounge chair and meditate on how I will become a better citizen when I return home, after vacation. I pull up the gossip magazine for cover and peer through my sunglasses at the Frenchwoman who is sunbathing topless, as some Frenchwomen do. Her taut breasts are bronzed, not a tan line in sight. I hesitate over taking my top off but as I peer down into my one-piece suit, all I can see is several hundred square centimeters of milky white skin. And my own chest isn't as chipper as hers.

On the third day we do laundry while the men play *pétanque.* As the women work, the French children do intricate crafts while mine throw Play-Doh at each other.

The Frenchwoman collects the sheets from the washing machine and hangs them on the line, straightening and pulling the cotton-linen blend tight. Snapping a clothespin at each end, she exclaims, *"Impeccable."* The sheets begin to dry while the surrounding fragrance of wild thyme and rosemary infuses the fab-

ric. When they are completely dry she gathers the scented sheets
to press with a hot iron.

While I had not planned on doing laundry on this short trip,
I act as if cleaning the sheets were on my agenda as well. Seeing
the line was taken by the Frenchwoman, I throw our covers into
the dryer and try to remember to pull them out promptly to
avoid wrinkles. As you can imagine, I forget.

Bedtime arrives and the French mom retrieves a pressed pa-
jama from her child's miniature suitcase. I take the cue and go
searching through our family's group duffel bag for a mismatched sweat suit for my son, and grab a T-shirt and leggings
for my daughter. The children safely tucked into bed, we retreat
to the dining room.

At the dinner table the Frenchwoman answers, *"Un tout petit
peu, s'il vous plaît,"* when my husband offers her an aged Burgundy wine. My eyes grasp for contact with his as I tap my finger
to the rim of the glass, silently insisting, *"Encore!"*

I study the Frenchwoman, whose makeup looks perfectly
natural. I pinch my cheeks for color and wet my lips while glaring at the thin woman with the tight black knit top and plunging
neckline. I unbutton a few buttons on my wrinkly jean top and
casually pull my bra straps up for effect. My husband shakes his
head, winks at me, and mouths, "I love you."

There is another verb tense in the French language, known as
the future perfect, and I think that is more my style.

REFERENCES: *à la fraise* = with strawberry; *un tout petit peu* = just a little bit; *encore* = more

Joaillier

(zhwahl-yay)

noun, masculine

jeweler

In *printemps* 1994 my fiancé, Jean-Marc, had whisked me through the streets of Torino, Italy, in search of the *bague*.

Unlucky *chez les joailleries italiennes,* and now back in his hometown of Marseilles, we scoured the streets of Rue Saint-Ferréol, drooling in boutiques such as Pellegrin and Frojo, looking for the right ring. I had one request (even before diamonds—what was I thinking?): that the ring be *platine*.

To my surprise, France didn't do platinum. Baffled, I asked the *joaillière*, "*Pourquoi?*" Unable to respond clearly, she said, "Doctors wear platinum," giving me reason to add one more French enigma to my growing list.

I remain perplexed (a state of mind I have since cultivated), and the white-gold ring on my left ring finger continues to take on a yellow hue as the years pass, but the memories of running through the streets of two major European cities in search of the *bague* are pure platinum.

REFERENCES: *le printemps* (m) = spring; *la bague* (f) = the ring; *chez les joailleries italiennes* = at the Italian jewelry shops; *une joaillerie* (f) = jewelry store; jewelry; *le platine* (m) = platinum; the feminine of *joaillier* is *joaillière; pourquoi?* = why?

Lâcher

(la-shay)

to let oneself go

In a quiet *crique* not far from Saint-Tropez, Jean-Marc, Max, Jackie, and I shared a memorable *dimanche après-midi* with friends from our village. The endless blue sky, crisp mistral wind, and abundant Mediterranean sun whispered to us, *"Profitez bien!"* because fall was around the corner, and such warm and lazy days would soon come to an end.

A few of us hunted *oursins* right off the shore to have as an appetizer with chilled white wine. We scissored open the porcupine-like shells and scooped out the fine salty-sweet orange mousse to savor alone or atop a torn piece of baguette.

You might call the beach we were on *privé*. Private, not because we paid to enter it, but because some of us walked far enough to reach the empty cove, while the other half of our group joined us by boat.

"Those are *pins tordus*," my friend Barbara explained, pointing to the twisted trunks of the low-lying pine trees. The trees formed a backdrop to our *déjeuner sur le sable,* the sea a quiet blue audience.

"How do you say *étoile de mer* in English?" Barbara asked. We were inching out into the cold water, which warmed as our conversation advanced.

"Starfish," I answered.

"*Poisson étoile,*" Barbara replied, translating the English term back into her own language.

Surrounded by *étoiles de mer,* the deep-blue Mediterranean, and the *éclats de rire* coming from our children, I thought of the words *savoir vivre.* I asked Barbara about the term and what it meant to her.

She explained that there is *le savoir vivre*—which includes education and etiquette—but also *savoir vivre,* which has to do with knowing how to enjoy life.

"Like '*un petit café le jeudi matin,*'" I said, referring to our occasional Thursday-morning meetings at the café, "or '*un pique-nique à la plage,*' or . . .'" Searching for more examples, I realized that I had not stopped to listen to Barbara's answer. Had she answered?

I looked up to find her scaling the steep rock where our children had spent the early afternoon plunging into the salty waters below.

Next I saw my graceful, usually demure friend pausing thoughtfully above the Mediterranean Sea. There she stood in her pink two-piece *maillot,* wavy blond hair framing her face and a peaceful smile shining down on us.

"*Allez, maman!*" her nine-year-old son cheered.

"*Vas-y*, Barbara!" my son added. "*Ouaiiiii!*" said Jackie.

"*Mon Dieu!*" I whispered.

The next thing I knew she plunged off that cliff, to the cheers of the children below.

Three little heads turned my way. The oldest kid—my son, Max—spoke. "Loosen up, Mom. Come on, let yourself go!"

Savoir vivre. Certain concepts are better experienced than explained.

REFERENCES: *une crique* (f) = cove, bay; *le dimanche après-midi* (m) = Sunday afternoon; *profitez bien! (profiter)* = take advantage!; *sur le sable* (m) = on the sand; *un éclat de rire* (m) = burst of laughter; *un pique-nique* (m) = picnic; *à la plage* = at the beach; *un maillot (de bain)* (m) = bathing suit; *allez, maman!* = go for it, Mom!; *vas-y* = go ahead; *ouaiiiii!* = yessss!; *mon Dieu* = my goodness

Expressions

lâcher prise = to let go, to lose one's hold

lâche-moi les baskets! = get off my back!

lâcher des sous = to fork out money

lâcher le morceau = to tell the truth, to come clean

lâcher le peloton = to get a lead on (the rest of the pack)

lâcher la bride à quelqu'un = to give someone more of a free rein

Lancer

(lon-say)

to throw

For Max's tenth birthday we enjoyed a bottle of Champomy—
the apple-juice-based, nonalcoholic "champagne" for kids.

Évidemment, Max wanted to pop the cork. *"S'il te plaît!"* he
pleaded. When Jean-Marc agreed, our son pointed the bottle
toward the unsuspecting ficus tree and prepared to launch the
bouchon.

"Non, Max!"

Jean-Marc demonstrated to Max how to grip the cork before
easing it out thanks to a series of gentle to-and-fro twists of the
bottle.

When Max warned that he was about to *"faire péter le bouchon,"* Jackie and I looked at each other, faces reddening. That's
when my seven-year-old corrected her brother.

"It's not *péter,* Max. It's *lancer.*"

Max was oblivious to his sister's comment, concentrating instead on the bottle, which was now giving up its cork.

I could see what Jackie meant; *péter* (pronounced *peh-tay*) can be an embarrassing verb, depending. While it does mean to pop, to burst, to snap, or to bust, *péter* also means to pass gas. Jackie's verb, *lancer*, was a bit more refined.

Until recently, I thought the verb *péter* had only one meaning—the face-reddening one. Then last summer, at a kilometer-long table of French vacationers, the unshaven, swimsuit-clad Frenchman at the opposite end of the buffet shouted to me: *"Hey-oh! Fais péter le pain!"*

My face turned *rouge-tomate* then, as well. You can imagine the translation going on in my head at the time: Hey, make that bread fart! I had the urge to tell the guy that we don't talk that way at the dinner table (or even away from the dinner table). Until I realized that he was speaking in slang—southern French argot at that. Without missing a beat, I made that bread *dart* across the table and was rewarded with an enthusiastic *"Merci, ma cocotte!"*—thanks, my little hen!

Finally, Max's phrase *péter le bouchon* makes perfect sense when you consider that the French call sparkling water "gassy water" *(eau gazeuse)*. As to champagne, it would follow that one is truly "passing gas" when popping that cork. With this information in mind, it'll be up to you to keep a straight face the next time you uncork a bottle of champers for your beloved.

REFERENCES: *le bouchon* (m) = cork; *faire péter le bouchon* = to pop the cork; *Hey-oh! Fais péter le pain!* = Hey! Pass the bread!

❧

Expressions

lancer une opération = to launch an operation

se lancer = to make a name for oneself; to give something a try

lance-toi! = Just do it! (to encourage someone who has a project)

Langue

(lahng)

noun, feminine

tongue

Bamboo, *lauriers-roses*, blackberries, and a hedge with orange-scented blossoms flank the stone *escalier* that we use to access the sandy beach.

Not far from a pile of dried seaweed I unfold two *serviettes de bain*, trying, within so many precious square meters, to respect the privacy of the young and amorous couple at the end of the beach.

I'm not sure what the name of the little *plage* is, or just exactly where we are. Jean-Marc has done the driving and, as usual, I have paid no attention to the road, but gotten lost in rolling vineyards and the sight of a cobalt blue sea.

Looking up I can see the restaurant Chez Camille. I do know we are just west of the famous jet-setty Pampelonne beach. To our right and just a few meters away is a rocky trail leading into the Mediterranean waters. Max and Jackie will spend hours searching through the rock pool, collecting hermit crabs and taking turns delivering fish bait to their father, who is perched on a far-off *rocher,* pole in hand.

I listen to an Englishman talk to his children. Though he is speaking in his native tongue, I know that he is living in France by the way he addresses his son. *Tee-mo-tay,* he says, instead of *Tim-oh-thee,* as it would be said in England. When his wife opens her mouth, French words come out, confirming my assumption.

I eavesdrop with envy as the man speaks, enunciating every English word, patiently guiding his bilingual toddler. I am interested to hear how the child will respond, and soon enough my curiosity is satisfied. The boy approaches the sunburned giant and says, "Daddy."

I try and remember the last time my kids called me Mommy. These days it's *maman.* My own speech is a garble of whatever language pops into my head and out of my mouth first. Most of the time I am not aware of which language I am speaking, until someone points it out: "How lucky your children are to hear you speak English!" the French will say. "What an advantage they'll have later on."

The truth is, Jackie and Max speak broken English— sometimes struggling for their words when it comes time to communicate with English speakers.

Somewhere along the line—specifically, the point at which communicating between cultures became a three-ring language circus as I tried to keep up a French conversation with the French while answering my children in English (tripping forward and backward, only to land in the pit that is Franglais)—I quit speaking English consistently to my children. This will not do. I will begin *aujourd'hui*—I mean: *I will begin today!*

REFERENCES: *le laurier-rose* (m) = oleander; *un escalier* (m) = stairway; *une serviette de bain* (f) = towel; *une plage* (f) = beach; *un rocher* (m) = rock, a boulder

· · · · · · · · · · · · · · · · · · · · · · ·

Expressions

la langue maternelle = mother tongue
la langue verte = slang
une mauvaise langue = a gossip
tenir sa langue = to keep a secret
donner sa langue au chat = to give up (while guessing)
avoir un cheveu sur la langue = to lisp
avoir la langue dans la poche = to keep one's opinions to
    oneself
tenir la langue = to stick out one's tongue (at someone)

Lécher

(lay-shay)

to lick

My French friends pronounce Cannes *can,* as in "a can of Spam" or "a cancan girl," and not *con,* like "pros and cons" or "chili con carne."

Funnily enough, you won't find a lot of cancan girls in Cannes (or chili con carne, for that matter), but you will find *beaucoup de boutiques* along Rue d'Antibes; and such is our quest on a sunny Friday *matin* in June.

The *rues,* or streets, in Cannes are *propres,* as are the *bâtiments.* Brigitte says that the façades are *belles* and I look up, wondering if such a style is Baroque or neo-Gothic (words I've just seen in a guidebook). Though I can spot a Balzac or a Flaubert a few bookshelves away, architecture is not my forte.

"J'adore l'odeur de la mer!" Barbara says as we amble along Rue d'Antibes and, with that, I look down a side street, to a great splash of turquoise sea. I too love the scent of the Mediterranean

and so I sniff, trying with all my might to smell the sea breeze. I can't, but say *"Oui!"* anyway.

We are in Cannes "licking windows," to borrow the funny French phrase *faire du lèche-vitrines*, the nonliteral translation being "window-shopping."

We enter a boutique, and when my friend disappears behind the dressing room curtain, I begin to wonder about my shop-ping-with-French-friends etiquette: Should I wait two minutes outside the dressing room, then say, "Come on out, let's see?" Or do I remain discreet, and let my French friend make up her own mind? I try out both etiquettes, intermittently waiting by the curtain, offering, *"Ça va?"* then dashing to the opposite end of the boutique, casually flipping through a rack of clothing.

In another shop, I try on white shorts and decide that French etiquette must be to leave the tryer-on-er in peace, because when I peek out the dressing room window, my friends are at the other end of the shop.

I ask them to please come over. Brigitte looks at me in the shorts and says, matter-of-factly: "They also come in beige or pink."

"That means you don't like the white?" I say.

"I didn't say that, it's just for your information."

"The white doesn't look good then?"

Brigitte's silence makes me want to hide behind the *rideau*, but it's too late now, she's about to speak. Pointing to my legs, she says: "If you want the white shorts, then you'd better show those some sun."

I back into the *cabine* for cover. So much for cancan girl legs.

REFERENCES: *le matin* (m) = morning; *propre* = clean; *un bâtiment* (m) = building; *belle* = beautiful; *le rideau* (m) = curtain; *une cabine (d'essayage)* (f) = dressing room

Expressions

une lèche-botte = a bootlicker
le lèche-vitrines = window-shopping
faire du lèche-vitrines = to go window-shopping
s'en lécher les babines = to lick one's lips
se lécher les doigts = to lick one's fingers
trop léché = overdone, overpolished

Linge

(lanzh)

noun, masculine

laundry

Three Americans—*une New-Yorkaise, une Texane,* and *une Phoeniciane*—transplanted to France commiserate. The subject: *le linge;* more precisely, the washing of it. We learn that each of us, at one point or another, has tried introducing a blanket into a French washing machine. The result is the same: the *couvertures,* even the thinnest of them, just don't fit into French washers.

The answer: *le pressing*—a jaw-dropping solution at almost 20 euros per washed blanket. It almost makes more sense to just buy a new one. Of course, there are the economical coin-operated *launderettes,* if you are lucky enough to have one in your village.

As we complain about French *électroménager,* my husband can't resist: "But didn't you know?" he says with a grin. "It is the *Moyen-Âge* in France!"

Six kohl-lined eyes dart his way. We washerwomen are not so amused by his comment, as it does not solve our dilemma.

"Do y'all have a clothes dryer?" *la Texane* says, referring to what has been, up until recently, a novel item in France. *Étonnant*, considering the first clothes dryers were invented by the French before 1800.

"I have a dryer!" *la New-Yorkaise* confirms.

"So do I!" says *moi, la Phoeniciane*

Jean-Marc pipes back in: "Even in *Arizona* they have clothes dryers. They have a whole *Desert* to dry the clothes, but noooo—they need an electric machine for that!"

We women sigh and return to our conversation.

"My dryer holds only three kilos, so I have to hang out the other two kilos," says *la New-Yorkaise*, explaining that her prized and rare American-size washing machine can hold a record five kilos, or eleven pounds, of *linge*. (The French salesman tried to talk her out of buying the monster. "What on earth could you need such a big washing machine for?" he wondered.)

There are Frenchwomen I know who iron their sheets—and sometimes their children's underwear!—meticulously folding the linen before stacking it in neat miniature towers in a lavender-scented armoire.

Though some of us have dryers, we still use a lot of clothes-pins, or *pinces à linge*, opting to use the electric drying machine only when the rain pours down. These days, I find there is nothing more pleasant than laundry that is naturally dried, literally infused with the scent of surrounding lavender, rosemary, fennel, or thyme.

That said, this French fervor for linen care—and the idea of keeping up with the French in the laundry room—left me intimidated at first, downright rebellious at times, so that only in the most pressing circumstances could I be found iron-in-hand. Jean-Marc seemed to have accepted his fate as the rare Frenchman in a wrinkled shirt.

That is, until recently. At the mega *supermarché* in Marseilles, while perusing the *électroménager* department, I told him, "We need a new iron."

Our iron has literally collected dust for ten years so that when it does occur to me to press something the fabric is eventually stained by the buildup on the iron's surface. Normally I just iron stuff inside out so that if a mark does appear it shows on the inside of the garment. Enough of that, I reason—time to change irons.

162

Back at the *électroménager* aisle, my husband stands silent, stunned by my comment. "I wanted to buy a new one years ago," he finally admits, "but I didn't want to offend you."

REFERENCES: *une New-Yorkaise* = woman from New York; *une Texane* = woman from Texas; *une Phoeniciane* = woman from Phoenix; *le pressing* (m) = dry cleaner's; *une launderette* (f) = Laundromat; *l'électroménager* (m) = electrical appliances; *le Moyen-Âge* = Middle Ages; *étonnant(e)* = surprising

Also

le linge de table = table linen

laver/étendre le linge = to wash/hang out the laundry

être blanc comme un linge = to be as white as a sheet

le beau linge = posh, upper-crust people

Il faut laver son linge sale en famille. = Don't air your dirty laundry in public.

. . . .

Machin

(mah-shun)

noun, masculine

thingamajig, whatchamacallit

French bathrooms are strange to begin with, and in most homes a separate tiny chamber is reserved just for the pot. There isn't much to do in a two-foot-by-four-foot closet unless you happen to be a curious *invitée*. On this particular day, at a new friend's house, when I was safely locked behind the door of the *petit coin*, my eyes locked on a strange object coming out of the wall, just inches from the floor.

I leaned in closer to inspect what by now I was sure was some sort of scent-distributing *machin*, only couldn't figure out how it worked. I pushed at it, then pulled, then pushed again, somewhat worried I'd break it but too curious to stop. I kept trying until . . .

If you've ever been shot in the head at point-blank range by a small one-ounce plastic contraption bursting with potent distilled air freshener, then you can appreciate the shock I endured.

The jet of flowery perfume just missed my eye but made a grand splash along the left side of my head, effectively depleting what volume I had tried to coax into my hair that morning. I exited the toilet sporting a forest-fresh scent, this curious *invitée* now wondering about how to explain the cloud of air freshener following her back to the dining table.

REFERENCE: *un invité (une invitée)* = guest

· · · · · · · · · ❧ · · · · · · · · · ·

Expressions

Machin = Mr. What's-His-Name
Machine = Mrs. What's-Her-Name

Manquer
(mahn-kay)

to miss

$\mathcal{P}$eople often ask, "Do you miss the States?" or, *"Ça vous manque les États-Unis?"* And I am troubled by the absence (or *manque*) of that emotional tug in response to the question. The truth is, no. I don't miss the States.

If you had asked me that question two or three months into my expatriation, I would have said *(sans hésitation)*, "Do I ever!"

Strangely, I missed things before I missed people. I missed peanut butter, Carmex, cranberry juice, the freeway, shower curtains, wall-to-wall carpeting, 100 percent cotton, salted popcorn, ice cubes, happy hour, rectangular pillows, air-conditioning, Thanksgiving, the twenty-four-hour convenience store, the Arizona monsoon . . . I don't miss those things anymore (except for monsoon season). *Pas du tout.*

Instead, I miss my grandma, who just turned eighty-five.

We had the chance to visit Grandma Audrey on our last visit to the States. We flew into Salt Lake City and drove to her vil-

lage, located about forty-five minutes from the capital. The
most cozy and comfortable environment I know is *chez ma
grand-mère.* I love to open her cupboards and *coffres* and find all
of the *bricoles* and *bibelots* she has collected since she was a young
bride. I love to curl up on her couch, with one of her handmade
afghans for cover, and examine the objects I used to marvel over
as a three-year-old, back at the trailer park in Bouse, Arizona.
"If you get tired, hon, you can take a nap," she still says.

Chez ma grand-mère, we drink weak coffee with thick cream
and she'll say, "Did you get something to eat this morning,
Heidi? Julie? I mean, Kristi?"

There is always comfort food at my grandmother's: fried potatoes, milk, jarred peaches, Cheez Whiz, turkey burritos, and of
course, *bonbons.*

I love to hear her say, "He's a Marcus!" when she looks at my
son. Here in France, I am used to hearing, "He looks just like his
oncle Jacques!" or, "She resembles her *tante* Cécile!" I want to hear
someone remark, "I see Uncle Rusty!" or, "She gets that from her
aunt Reta." Nobody says that here. *Jamais.*

I miss America when the plane descends into Phoenix and
the lights on Camelback Mountain come into view. When the
plane hits the runway at the Sky Harbor Airport my heart is instantly in my throat: excitement mixed with the feeling that I
have never left home. I look up to find that the passengers are
now wearing ASU T-shirts. Someone has a roadrunner on her
pastel-toned sweatshirt and people are wearing tennis shoes.

When I leave Nice, France, for the twenty-hour voyage west,
the passengers are wearing black, and bidding loved ones

farewell: *"Je t'aime. À très bientôt!"* they say. They drink Côtes du Rhône red wine, which helps camouflage the bad taste of the items on the cramped fold-down trays before them.

But the passengers who disembark in Phoenix say things like, "Hey, guy, take it easy," or, "Now, you have a nice time with your granddaughter. Take care."

I miss America now, as I type this last line. It's in the sting of my eyes, the lump in my throat. Would somebody please ask me if I miss the States? I can answer that now.

REFERENCES: *pas du tout* = not at all; *chez ma grand-mère* = at my grandmother's home; *un coffre* (m) = chest; *une bricole* (f) = trifle, trinket, token; *un bibelot* (m) = a knickknack; *un oncle* (m) = uncle; *une tante* (f) = aunt; *jamais* = never, ever; *je t'aime* = I love you; *à très bientôt!* = see you real soon!

Expressions

manquer sa vie = to make a mess of one's life

manquer une occasion = to miss an opportunity

manquer à sa parole = to break one's word

manquer à son devoir = to fail in one's duty

manquer à une règle = to violate a rule

manquer à quelqu'un = to be disrespectful to somebody

Marchander

(mar-shan-day)

to bargain

The *artisan's* drill ground my nerves along with whatever else he was pulverizing in the next room. I have taken for granted the peace and quiet of this country abode; leave it to a home repair visit to get me thinking about gratitude.

I hadn't expected to come into contact with Monsieur l'Artisan. I thought my husband had settled the account and that all I had to do was type away in the next room, and sort of *be present* in case of a question or to lock up afterward. So when the *artisan* tapped on my window, I waved, mouthing, *"Merci, monsieur. Au revoir!"*

When Monsieur remained at the window, I reluctantly got up to open it.

"Check, please!" His request startled me and then I realized Jean-Marc had, in fact, not paid for the work. Before I could respond, *"Combien ça fait?"*—how much?—he replied, *"Cinq cent cinquante."*

"Five hundred and fifty euros!"

"*Oui*," came the verdict. I hesitated long enough for him to add: "Does that sound like a lot?"

"Why, it's almost as much as I earn in a month at my part-time job at the vineyard!"

This caused the *artisan* to shake his head and raise his shoulders, a mix of pride and contempt. At least I was exaggerating, I reassured myself.

"*Allez*, four hundred and fifty euros," he bargained.

"But how much does that come to an hour?" I said, buying time until I could think of what to do next.

He evaded. "I don't work by the hour . . . *Allez*, three hundred and fifty euros! We'll forget about tax."

"Sold!"

170

REFERENCE: *un artisan* (m) = craftsman, skilled worker

Expression

savoir marchander = to know how to bargain

Maudit

(mo-dee)

cursed

$\mathcal{I}$ was beginning to believe that we were cursed but brushed it off to paranoia. Then the other day, over lunch, Jean-Marc confirmed my suspicion. *"On est maudit,"* he said.

It wasn't a bad curse, as curses go; we were—*tout simplement*—cursed in our efforts to have a basketball hoop *chez nous*. Not that we didn't try. (The outer wall of our house now has a basketball-size crater to prove it.) Jean-Marc had previously installed a hoop with a heavy metal rim to the rock wall. First, he drilled holes into the layered rock siding. When that didn't work, he pierced holes into the plaster between the rocks. When the hoop came crashing down, it took with it several of the old stones. After two or three *tentatives* at attaching the hoop to the wall, we were about to abandon our plans. That's when my husband discovered another system: the "portable" *panier*.

On Saturday, Jean-Marc stood in the driveway amid a jumble of basketball hoop parts. His mission: to assemble the portable basketball system in time for our son's upcoming tenth birthday. Thirty minutes into the *assemblage* I could hear him cursing the basketball gods. Attacking the thirteenth page of the instruction booklet, he cried out: *"Tu peux venir m'aider?"* Can you come here and help me?

My job was to hold or insert pieces (or to do both simultaneously). First, I balanced the heavy plastic base of the portable basketball system while Jean-Marc tried to insert a heavy three-meter pole, connecting a dangling bolt with a hard-to-see, impossible-to-reach eyehole.

"C'est une blague!"—it's a joke!—I said to Jean-Marc on our third attempt. He shook his head in frustration.

We decided to reread the instruction booklet. We read it in French. Then in English. Then in French again. We compared notes and realized that the instructions made absolutely no sense in Jean-Marc's language or mine. "Well, you speak Spanish, don't you? Maybe we should try the *espagnole* version," I said, flipping through the instruction booklet and going down the line of possibilities, which included Swedish and German. "That won't work either—because all of these instructions have been translated from Chinese!" Jean-Marc said, throwing the booklet aside.

They were of no use to us, even if we could speak German or Swedish or even Chinese. As a sometime translator, having personally decoded technical documents before, I could imagine a low-paid worker in some dimly lit, cramped office guessing her way through parts vocabulary and verbs dealing with twisting, tightening, and tilting. I felt compassion for her, even if I did want to wring her neck.

Next it began to rain.

When *cordes* of rain fell from the sky, the heavy three-meter pole was not completely secured and we were missing one of four metal nuts. I reached down to turn Jean-Marc's collar up so he wouldn't get drenched. When buckets of rain began to flood the driveway and the instructions floated off, we gathered the remaining pocket-size parts and scrambled inside.

The next day, five of us—including Max, Jackie, and our friend Pierre—completed the assembly of the portable basketball hoop. Sans instructions, this time.

REFERENCES: *on est maudit* = we are cursed; *tout simplement* = quite simply; *chez nous* = at our place, home; *une tentative* (f) = attempt; *un assemblage* (m) = assembly; *une corde* (f) = rope (Here: torrents. The noun is taken from the expression *il pleut/il tombe des cordes* = it's raining cats and dogs.)

Also

le Maudit = the devil
les maudits = the damned

Expressions

Maudit! (expletive) = Damn it!
être en maudit = to be angry
Quel maudit temps! = What lousy weather!
Maudit soit le jour où . . . = Cursed be the day when . . .

Ménage

(may-nazh)

noun, masculine

housework

What's foreign can be off-putting, and at times a word is a three-eyed monster. French words baffled me for years. Now English words intimidate my children and, in some cases, are downright confusing—at least from the look on my son's face.

"*Deesh-wah-share?*" he repeats after me.

Max sits for a moment, considering my request, and then darts out of the *salon*. I begin to clear the breakfast table, piling boxes of cereal under my left arm, stacking bowls with my right. On my way to the kitchen I stop before the TV, lift my right toe to the screen, and turn off the morning cartoons.

Once in the kitchen, and with no sign of Max and a full dishwasher in sight, I shrug. I realize he must have been fleeing the scene—rather than hurrying to help.

Trying to get a few chores done before noon, I continue with the *ménage,* picking up an orphaned shoe here, a glue cap there, and candy wrappers . . . everywhere! *"Hey-oh!"* I say, discovering the evidence. "No snacking before lunch!" I toss the crinkled foils into the *poubelle* and head to the washing machine.

Meeting Jackie in the hall, I say: "Would you please get the *balai* and sweep your room? Thanks!" I squeeze her rubber-duck belly to release a few giggles from her beak. *"Allez!"* I say, and head to the bathroom.

Entering the *salle de bains,* where we keep our washing machine, I find Max crouched to the floor, pulling damp clothes from the *lave-linge.* Like most French washing machines, the door is on the front side of the machine, just inches from the ground.

"Max! What are you doing?" I say.

"You said to empty the *wah-share,*" he explains.

"The *dish-wah-share!* You know—forks, knives, cups . . ."

"Ah, *le lave-vaisselle,*" he translates, and heads off in the direction of the *cuisine.*

Poor little guy with the foreign mommy, I think as I set the plastic laundry basket on the floor, empty the *wah-share,* and head outside to hang the *linge.*

175

REFERENCES: *la poubelle* (f) = garbage can; *le balai* (m) = broom; *la salle de bains* (f) = bathroom; *le lave-linge* (m) = washing machine; *le lave-vaisselle* (m) = dishwasher; *la cuisine* (f) = kitchen

Expressions

le grand ménage = spring cleaning

faire le ménage = to do the housework

faire du ménage dans sa vie = to sort one's life out

la scène de ménage = a row (as when couples blow up publicly)

se mettre en ménage = to get married, to live as a married couple

le ménage à trois = household of three

faire bon/mauvais ménage avec quelqu'un = to get along well/badly with someone

Mendiant

(mon-dee-ahn)

noun, masculine

beggar

The first time I saw him he was zigzagging across the two-lane street, just in front of the Bar des Sports. Though he was walking alone, his lips were moving as if in dialogue and his arms, which flailed, seemed to underline his point.

I carefully sidestepped him whenever we shared the same sidewalk. And then my mom had her accident and came to live with me in France. As she healed, she took to going to the cafés. Before long, she knew most of the characters in our village.

I avoided going to the cafés with my mom because she loved to talk to those around us: the street beggar, the prostitute, the town drunk, and all of the characters in between. I had nothing against these people; I just didn't want to get involved with them. "This is my village!" I told her, reminding her that she would be boarding a plane home in no time, but that I'd have to deal with all these people she was inviting into our lives.

And then she got cancer. She stayed on for another year or so, trying to heal. She continued to go to the cafés. I joined her.

Soon enough we ran into Zigzag.

"Come on over, Jean! Would you like a coffee?" my mother called to him.

"Mom!" I whispered.

"Oh, what are you worried about?"

"*Salut,*" said Jean, kissing her on both cheeks. "How are you feeling?" he asked, tapping his chest. I noticed how he spoke English with my mom, and spoke it well.

He wagged a finger at my mom. "No cigarettes!"

"This is my last one," she said.

I rolled my eyes.

Zigzag, or Jean, never drank coffee in the morning. "Not before my pastis and steak tartare," he added.

Well, there you go! I thought. Pastis in the morning!

Zigzag didn't join us. Perhaps he sensed my malaise. Instead he stood at the counter, forking steak tartare into his mouth. I noticed his gray mustache—the only place on his head where hair seemed to grow, besides his jet-black eyebrows.

"I never have pastis before some steak! The steak lines the stomach!" he said. I looked at my watch, which read 8:45 AM.

The fire would happen later, leaving Jean homeless and half dead. He disappeared for quite a few months, emerging in late spring, this time in a wheelchair. He could not push himself, but was accompanied by someone. I think it was his brother. He looked lost and was as pale as his favorite pastis. I wasn't certain he was all there and once again I took to avoiding him; I told myself that he probably didn't recognize me anyway. In truth, I just didn't know what to say. My mom, who would have, had gone home to Mexico.

Month after month I saw him wheeled through the village. I watched him closely, even though I didn't speak to him. I was afraid he was dying.

The other morning, after dropping the kids at school, I drove through the village and stopped at the crosswalk, that same place where I saw Zigzag for the first time.

Would you believe he was standing? Yes, right there outside the Bar des Sports. He gripped a cane in his right hand and with his left he waved, looking me in the eye and smiling warmly. On the table just behind him lay a small tray of steak tartare and a tumbler of pastis.

Moelle

(mwal)

noun, feminine

marrow

On the seventh of January the Niçois were peeling off jackets, scarves, and *gilets* to lunch in T-shirts along the *place*. And so was I.

Normally I should have been *chez moi*, behind a computer screen, fretting about *l'orthographe*, but Jean-Marc and I had driven to Nice for the day.

Along the Promenade des Anglais, people Rollerbladed or walked aimlessly. *"Quel beau temps!"* they said.

At the restaurant where we stopped to have lunch, I inquired about the *soupe du jour*.

"We don't have soup," the waiter replied. "In France, we don't specialize in soup. Maybe in Holland or Germany, but not France." His empty stare shot up several inches and he fixed his eyes on the square, tapping his pencil against his notepad.

His response hit me like an artillery of frozen clam shells. It's not the fact that he pegged me as a foreigner. It's just the idea that, go where I may, there's a bright blinking *panneau* that I lug with me, slapped to my forehead. It reads: *"Étrangère."* Sometimes I just want to unplug it and leave it behind, and be able to say things like: "Monsieur, have you not heard of consommé?" or, "Does *soupe au pistou* ring a bell?" or, "Then just what *is* the purpose of croutons, *après tout?*"

But sarcasm does not suit me, and it won't change the *menu du jour*.

Jean-Marc ordered the *pot-au-feu avec son os à moelle* and I asked for *fricassée de poulpe*.

When the waiter left, my husband shook his head. "In France we don't specialize in soup." What's that supposed to mean?"

After lunch, Jean-Marc and I made our way down the narrow stairs to the seashore, where the French draped themselves across the white pebble beach. Some people were taking a siesta and some even swimming in the Mediterranean. One couple did yoga. A woman wrote in a diary. Several men read *Nice-Matin*. I lay on my back, having rearranged the pebbles beneath just so.

Slumber reached me from beneath the *soleil du midi* and, still bugged about the waiter's comment, I fell asleep with these words on my lips:

In France we don't specialize in soup. Pfft. . . .
In New York we don't do bagels.
In Maine we don't have lobster.
In Iowa, corn—ça n'existe pas.

In Florida we don't have grapefruit.
In Louisiana we don't do gumbo.
In Idaho, pas de patates.
In Arizona we don't . . . In Arizona we don't . . . In Arizona . . .

REFERENCES: *un niçois (une niçoise)* = person from Nice; *un gilet* (m) = cardigan; *la place* (f) = public square; *l'orthographe* (f) = spelling; *quel beau temps!* = what a beautiful day!; *la soupe du jour* (f) = the soup of the day; *le panneau* (m) = sign; *la soupe au pistou* = vegetable soup with basil and garlic; *après tout* = after all; *le pot-au-feu avec son os à moelle* = stew of vegetables and beef with its bone marrow; *la fricassée* (f) *de poulpe* = octopus stew; *ça n'existe pas* = it doesn't exist; *pas de patates* = no spuds

182

Also

la moelle de bœuf = beef marrow
la moelle épinière = spinal marrow
la moelle osseuse = bone marrow

Expressions

corrompu jusqu'à la moelle = rotten to the core
n'avoir pas de moelle dans les os = to be weak
se ronger les moelles = to worry a lot
tirer la moelle = to extract the essential in something
sucer la moelle de quelqu'un = to suck the marrow from
    someone = to ruin someone

Morceau

(mor-so)

noun, masculine

piece

We had planned to see Versailles on our last day in Paris, but when Jean-Marc suggested we discover a *village typique* in Burgundy instead, the palatial, gold-plated Versailles quickly dulled. A soft-spoken French village with a *grand-mère* on the front porch feeding a day-old baguette to the pigeons, with country folk anchored to the benches along the narrow main road, with dilapidated shutters and crumbling façades— beautiful as they can only be in a foreign country—that is pomp and circumstance to me.

Coasting into the historic town of Avallon, I began to hum the Bryan Ferry song of the same name. "I don't think it's the same Avallon," Jean-Marc pointed out. I didn't think so either, if only because of the extra *l* in the town's name.

We were in town only for a quick stopover, and to *manger un morceau* as part of our eight-hour ride home from the capital. After lunch in a smoky brasserie we sauntered along the uneven cobblestone paths throughout the village. Near the church I steadied the window of my pocket-size automatic camera, using the old French door frame in the distance as a guide. Click . . . *Mince!* Out of space. Realizing there was no more available space on my memory card, I began to edit out photos, throwing images into the camera's virtual *poubelle,* agonizing over the loss as I tried to make room for Avallon.

Having created three or four more picture slots, I set out to rearrange the subject matter. I pushed a garbage can out of the way and rolled the portable NO PARKING sign off to the side, only to become frustrated at the sight of modern automobiles in front of the old, fading French doors. The cars would have to stay.

A cluster of teenagers seated along the stone wall paused to watch the *étrangère* rearrange a pocket of their village. As I looked ahead to the medieval church, they looked ahead too. When I set my sights to the crumbling turret, they directed their eyes up to the pointed head of its tower as well, mumbling something along the lines of, *"C'est vrai*—it's true that this is kind of a cool place." The blur of their hometown was now coming into focus.

Soon I ran out of space on the camera again. As I went over the images, viewing a half dozen morsels of Avallon, not sure of which to keep and which to destroy, I paused to look up at the teenagers, who sat silent, still experiencing the beautiful façade before them.

It was then that the words of Erik Orsenna echoed through my mind, causing me to return my camera to my front pocket: *"La vie est une. Qui la découpe en petits morceaux n'en peut saisir le visage."*

Life is one. Whoever cuts it into little pieces cannot grasp its face.

REFERENCES: *un village typique* (m) = characteristic village; *manger un morceau* = to have a quick bite to eat; *mince!* = darn!

Expressions

avaler le morceau = to swallow the bad news
couper/mettre/réduire en morceau = to break to pieces, to destroy
emporter le morceau = to succeed, to get one's own way
lâcher/cracher le morceau = to confess, to spill the beans
tomber en morceau = to fall to pieces
le morceau de vie = slice of life
mâcher les morceaux à quelqu'un = to chew the pieces for someone = to prepare the job/way for someone

Mort

(mohr)

noun, feminine

death

$\mathcal{A}$t the *cimetière* in the town of Fuveau, Jean-Marc hands Max, Jackie, and me roses that he has carefully cut from our *jardin.* *"Quelle couleur?"* he says. I choose *la jaune.*

We walk to the back of the cemetery, past rows of elaborate tombstones, some veritable chapels with elaborate statues out front and signs such as *"Famille Lefavre"* and *"Famille Gassin."*

We stop before a discreet granite block marked *"Famille Espinasse."* We each lay a rose atop the sand-colored gravestone, then stand silent. I notice that Jean-Marc rearranges the roses.

Max wonders why his family tombstone doesn't have photos like the others. In France, it is not uncommon to place a concrete "book" with the deceased's photo on one "page." The opposite page reads: *"À Ma Mémé Chérie"* or *"À Mon Papa Adoré."* The tomb we stand before has no headstone. It is flat, clear of books, ceramic roses, and not a miniature statue in sight. I had never before noticed the austerity of the Espinasse family tombstone, and find it *paisible*.

My husband explains to our children who the various family members are. "That's Papa Jacques," he says, pointing to one line on a list of names. "You see, I didn't know my grandfather either." I notice the last date next to Papa Jacques' name: 1967, which corresponds to the year of Jean-Marc's birth. Jean-Marc's father's name is the second to the last on the list: *"Gérard Espinasse 1937–1985."*

I feel the familiar chill, and then the sting coming from my eyes. I never knew Jean-Marc's father, only the lingering sadness in his children's regard.

Jean-Marc carefully clears the grounds directly around the tombstone, collecting an old planter and pulling out a few *mauvaises herbes* that have sprung up since our last visit.

187

On the horizon I see the majestic Mont Sainte-Victoire mountain range, the inspiration of painters such as Paul Cézanne. The cemetery is silent but for the thoughts of a six-year-old girl musing about her *grand-père: "C'est le papa de tout le monde,"* Jackie says, gripping my hand. He's everybody's papa, in her mind.

REFERENCES: *un cimetière* (m) = cemetery; *quelle couleur?* = what color?; *le jaune* (m) = yellow; *ma mémé chérie* (f) = my dear grandmother; *mon papa adoré* (m) = my adored father; *paisible* = peaceful; *une mauvaise herbe* (f) = weed

Expressions

être mort = to be exhausted
une ville morte = a ghost town
l'eau morte = stagnant water
la morte-saison = off season
un silence de mort = a deathly silence
la mort dans l'âme = heavy heart; heartache

Naître

(neh-tre)

to be born

The September of Jackie's birth sweltered in Cézanne's favorite city—especially if you were lugging around seventeen excess kilos. The maternity ward had no *climatisation,* so the women made do with open windows and magazine fanning.

"Please come out of there, Madame Espinasse! *Allez!*" the nurse called.

I had locked the bathroom door and was, as the nurse assumed, hiding out from the impending birth of my second child. The contractions were getting worse, but I did not feel ready for the event.

"I'm going to call the doctor if you don't come out of there, Madame Espinasse! *Allez! On y va!*"

Calling the doctor would be a good idea. My last run-in with childbirth in France, two years prior—for the birth of Max, in Marseilles—had the doctor arriving just in time to *couper le cordon.*

A few more threats and I was gradually lured out of the *WC.*

The nurse helped me back up onto the *table d'accouchement* before disappearing.

When the contractions became unbearable, I screamed for the *anesthésiste*. "It's too late for that now," the nurse said, popping her head around the corner.

In so many words, I made it crystal clear that, too late or not, the @ #! doctor would most certainly be giving me a *péridurale* or all *enfer* might just break loose.

If you think I was nervous, you haven't met Monsieur Espinasse, the nonsmoker who had just sprinted out of the delivery room to buy a pack of Gauloises, leaving me in the care of *l'infirmière d'enfer*.

My doctor, who not only resembled a French Eddie Murphy but was every bit as funny as the American *comédien*, burst through the door. *"Salut! Comment ça va?"*—Hey! How's it going?—he sang.

Things were much better now. And in the time it took to pull on plastic gloves and lift his mask, the baby was born.

The doctor was sewing up and telling jokes when I heard him say, "She . . ."

She!

I was so busy counting fingers and toes that I forgot to inquire about my child's gender.

"Le choix du roi," the nurse said, confirming that I now had a boy *and* a girl. The French call it "the king's choice."

I don't know about that, but I felt richer than a queen with a little strawberry blond girl safe in my arms.

REFERENCES: *un kilo* (m) = 2.2 pounds; *la climatisation* (f) = air-conditioning; *on y va!* = let's go!; *couper le cordon* = to cut the cord; *le WC* (m) = water closet, toilet; *la table d'accouchement* (f) = birthing table; *l'anesthésiste* (m, f) = anesthesiologist; *la péridurale* (f) = epidural; *l'infirmière d'enfer* (m) = nurse from hell; *le comédien* (m) = actor

Expressions

être né pour quelque chose = to be cut out for something
être né pour l'autre = to be made for each other
être né sous une bonne étoile = to be born under a lucky star
être né coiffé = to be born lucky
son pareil est à naître = his/her/its equivalent has yet to be born (when someone or something is unrivaled, matchless)

191

Pavillon

(pa-vee-yohn)

noun, masculine

bungalow

The dentist wrestled with the Mappy.fr website instructions, thrashing at the computer mouse, which shot back and forth like an air hockey mallet beneath his hand as he tried to click the right combination of icons that would produce the most user-friendly map.

His surgical mask lowered, eyes boring into the computer screen before him, he flustered. *"Ce n'est pas ça!"*—that's not it! More thrashing of the mouse ensued until the *imprimante* spit out a page titled *"Votre Itinéraire."* Not satisfied, he flipped the printout over, slapping it to the desk before drawing his own map: a fat column with a fork at the top. I was to stay to the right of the fork, and when the fork forked again, I was to keep to the left, following signs to Mourillon.

I am not at the dentist's office for an *arrachement d'une dent,* but to get driving instructions to Toulon. When I mentioned to my friend Brigitte that I was unsure about the best way to drive out to the coast, she insisted that I stop by the office and get instructions. I was sort of familiar with the Mappy.fr website but figured the dentist (who doubles as president of our town's ski club and its yearly voyage) knew the site best.

I thanked the dentist before Brigitte tucked a half dozen free samples into my pocket, including mouthwash and toothpaste, reminding me to take care of my *gencives*, which have been bothering me lately.

It takes forty-five minutes to get to Toulon from the town of Vidauban, where I enter the *autoroute*. I give myself two hours, *au cas où*. I've taken this road a hundred times—as a passenger—but it is only today that I discover it actually has a name: A 57. I follow the directions and am amazed at ending up at the southernmost point of France, a place where seagulls swirl above my head, *glycine* crawls along the rock walls of the homes perched above the sea, and an overall floral, humid air abounds.

I have ventured to Toulon to unwind at the end of the winding road that has led me to salty air and the cry of the *goéland*, to a *plage* called Mourillon. In a quaint neighborhood above the beach, I discover a hodgepodge of quirky villas, including that charming fits-like-a-glove-to-the-environment bungalow. Bungalow! I love the word, which is also used in French. The homes here are surrounded by faded wisteria, palm, and fragrant citrus trees, and other crawling, flowering, rustling, sweet-scented vegetation that I cannot identify. Some of the villas have enchanting names, such as *La Cigaloinette* and *Les Muguets*.

Zigzagging through the *voisinage*, I stumbled upon a street named Pourquoi Pas? and delighted in the fanciful appellation. Just to see the street sign again, I skipped to the end of the *rue* and snapped a photo of it there; behind the sign I glimpsed the irresistible bungalow with green shutters. *Quelle image.* I stood silent, smelling fragrant vines and salty air, listening to the sea, which transported me back to my room in Arizona, to my bed where I lay listening to the sound of waves that had been programmed into my clock radio as I fell asleep. There, I would dream of France, of when I would one day call her my home. When the doubting would begin, as it always did, I'd let the white noise of the clock radio, with its whoosh of the sea and intermittent cry of the seagull, drown out the negatives. When *le calme absolu* found me, the thought *"Pourquoi pas?"* would enter my mind. *"Pourquoi pas moi?"* I'd fall asleep to that question mark, and to France—always on my mind.

The cry of the *goéland* shook me from my reverie, and I opened my eyes and looked out to the navy blue French sea, pausing to acknowledge a dream come true.

I reached into my purse for my keys. It was time to go home now, back to my own bungalow in a cozy inland village where the sea's mist is known to influence the grapevines that sprout just outside my window as I type these last few words. Time to get my little Franco-Americans from school. I turned to take one last look at the charming *pavillon* tucked behind the amusing Pourquoi Pas? sign.

Pourquoi pas indeed.

REFERENCES: *une imprimante* (f) = printer; *un itinéraire* (m) = itinerary, route; *un arrachement d'une dent* = the pulling of a tooth; *les gencives* (f) = gums; *une autoroute* (f) = turnpike; *au cas où* = in case; *la glycine* (f) = wisteria; *le goéland* (m) = gull; *la cigaloinette* (from *cigale* = cicada) = cicada house; *le muguet* (m) = lily of the valley; *le voisinage* (m) = neighborhood; *quelle image* = what a sight; *le calme absolu* (m) = absolute calm; *pourquoi pas moi?* = why not me?

Also

un pavillon de banlieue = a suburban house
un pavillon de jardin = a summerhouse, pavilion
un pavillon de chasse = a hunting lodge
un pavillon de détresse = a distress flag

195

Expressions

amener son pavillon/baisser pavillon = to surrender
montrer son pavillon = to fight boldly
couler pavillon haut = to founder but not give up, to lose
   with elegance
se ranger sous le pavillon de quelqu'un = to put oneself
   under another's protection

Personnage

(pehr-so-nazh)

noun, masculine

character

Pressed to leave work at the vineyard and arrive on time to collect my children from school, I sped out of the company's parking lot and right into a roadblock. It wasn't a truck obstructing my path, but a farmer "doing his business."

The farmer looked up, nonchalant, then went back to matters pressing to him. As for *moi*, I put my car in reverse and found another path home.

· · · · · · · · · · ·  · · · · · · · · · · ·

Expressions

C'est un personnage! = She/he's quite a character!
jouer un personnage = to play a part, to act a part or role

· ·

Pétanque

(pay-tahnk)

noun, feminine

boules

"How would you like to proceed?" my guest asks me, the bungling hostess.

"Oh, you know, it's a buffet," I reply, pointing to a stack of paper plates.

"A buh-fay?" Pierre teases, until I suspect I have made another face-reddening linguistic gaffe, but don't dare ask which.

Atop a colorful Provençal tablecloth, an assortment of hors d'œuvres: roasted sweet red peppers in olive oil, pistachios, cucumber sticks, *saucissons,* chips, roasted nuts and olives, and two salads, Greek and pasta. On the grill: lamb chops and spicy *merguez* sausages.

When we finish the salads and grilled meat, I ask the *invités* if they would like dessert now, or after the *pétanque* tournament. *"Tout de suite, non?"*—why not right away—they say, and

I now understand that the stomach comes before *le sport* in France.

We eat a chilled salad of quartered oranges with cinnamon and sliced almonds and a homemade *gâteau au chocolat* while studying the diagram my husband has printed out; on it the teams are named and the match schedule is explained.

Jean-Marc has organized the teams as *Italie,* France, *Espagne, République Tchèque,* and *Angleterre* and included only one rule: "It is forbidden to throw the *boules* [heavy steel balls] at one another."

I try to follow the *pétanque* game, understanding a very few basics:

1. *Pétanque* (aka *boules*) is a game where you toss steel balls *(boules)* across a playing field, or *terrain,* toward a smaller ball, called a *cochonnet* (pig) or "jack," the object of it being to see who can get closest.
2. The game is played on a dirt *terrain,* or rectangular patch of ground.
3. It can be played one-on-one *(tête-à-tête)* or in teams of two or three. We are playing in *équipes,* or teams, of two, known as *doublettes.*

I notice there are some players who specialize in *tirage,* or shooting at the opponent's steel ball and knocking it from the *cochonnet,* and others in "pointing," that is, throwing the heavy ball closest to the *cochonnet.*

I hear a lot of *"Tire, tire!"* or *"Allez, pointe!"* from my nine-year-old teammate and son, Max, but I continue to throw the heavy steel sphere *"à ma façon,"* in my own way.

A general fuss ensues when it is time to count points. Certain "boulistes" measure *boule/cochonnet* distance by placing their shoe between the two, others insist you must use a long blade of grass for a measure. Arguing and cussing follow, until the players collect the *boules* and begin the next round.

After another round, when the arguing picks up again and the Frenchwomen begin to cuss like sailors, I remember the left-over chocolate cake and make a speedy *aller-retour* to the fridge. A little sugar, in my experience, always calms the *nerfs*.

REFERENCES: *le saucisson* (m) = (cold) sausage; *l'Espagne* (f) = Spain; *la (République) Tchèque* (f) = Czech Republic; *l'Angleterre* (f) = England; *un aller-retour* (m) = round trip; *un nerf* (m) = nerve

Piger
(pee-zhay)

to understand

$\mathcal{I}$ paused before my son's room, unsure about what sort of mood lingered behind the *porte*.

Once over the threshold, I was greeted with an enthusiastic *"Salut, maman!"*

"Hi, Max," I replied.

"J'ai tout pigé, maman!"—I understood everything!—he said, tapping the page in front of him.

Ouf. Two days ago it was a different story, one involving tears and a torn spirit. Max was having a fit: not an angry, violent rage, but a helpless, it's-all-too-much-for-me meltdown—not unusual for a nine-year-old *élève* with a formidable load of homework.

"What's wrong, Max?" I had said.

"Sans lignes!"

"I know, I know. I gave you the paper without lines—just what you asked for."

"Sans lignes!" he cried, red-faced and increasingly torn.

"Max! Here it is. Paper *without* lines. Calm down, OK?"

"Je dois écrire CENT *lignes, maman."* And with that, he crumpled to the floor, finally tucking his head into his lap after knocking it against his knees a few times.

Suddenly it became clear.

Cent, not *sans*—"one hundred" instead of "without."

Now Max's anguish made sense. I realized the teacher had once again asked him to write one hundred lines, as punishment for forgetting to bring home a certain textbook.

With another simple language misunderstanding cleared up, one of us felt much less frustrated; the other had a sore wrist to look forward to.

REFERENCES: *ouf!* = phew!; *sans lignes* = without lines; *je dois écrire cent lignes* = I have to write one hundred lines

Also

un(e) pigiste = pieceworker, typesetter, freelance journalist who is paid by the line

Expressions

tu piges? = get it?

pige-moi ça! = take a look at that!

je n'y pige rien = I just don't get it

n'y piger que dalle = to understand nothing

Plume
(ploom)

noun, feminine

feather

Out watering our lawn, I'm easily amused by the *arc-en-ciel* that appears when I tilt the spray at just the right angle beneath the *soleil du midi*. I enjoy standing out in the yard in the morning and in the evening, and find *l'arrosage* relaxing. To think that one year ago a muddy plot of land existed where wildflowers now push up and thrive amid a thickening *pelouse*.

My six-year-old runs out of the house and I check to see if she is ready for basketball practice: tennis shoes, T-shirt, *gourde*, and *plume* . . . *Plume!* For weeks she's carefully completed her look with a fuzzy lavender-colored feather in her hair. It looked like basketball practice would not deter her careful presentation.

"*Très jolie,*" I say, brushing wheat-colored hair from her shoulder before turning off the hose.

"I took them from my costume," Jackie replies.

"Them? You mean the one in your hair, right?"

"Oh, I lost yesterday's feather. I got another one off the costume."

I realize she's been snapping off a fresh new feather each day from the feather boa I bought her for *carnaval*.

If it isn't a feather to accentuate her look, it's a long velvet gown over jeans. *"Mais, il fait froid dehors!"* she complains, trying to get away with such a getup. Another ensemble she fancies includes a purple dance sarong over velvet multicolored leggings. "You can't wear that, Jackie, you're going to *les échecs!*" She promises the outfit is fine for *échecs*, and that she just won't wear it to school. *"D'accord, maman?"*

She gets these eccentricities from my side of the family, specifically from my mom. Seven years ago, in the village of Saint Maximin, Jackie's fifty-year-old grandmother-to-be turned heads under the August sun. My mom had come to France for the summer to await the arrival of her first *petite-fille*. The villagers came to know my mom as "Madame with spurs on her boots."

"Mom, why don't we go out and get you a pair of *espadrilles*?" I'd suggested, shifting my weight to accommodate an in utero Jackie.

"No thanks, sweetheart, I like my boots," she'd said, tucking in her new white souvenir T-shirt with *St-Tropez, Monaco,* and *Cannes* written across the front. She'd already ripped out the constrictive neck, all the better to accentuate strands of silver and turquoise beads; her long dark hair was twisted thick beneath a straw fedora. She'd tucked a feather or two into the hat-band as an afterthought. A style all her own. My daughter has such DNA. It must skip a generation.

I observe my little girl and wish I had the courage to stick a fuzzy lavender feather in my own hair. Instead I push wayward locks off my face, pull on loafers, smooth down an unremarkable outfit, and follow in my daughter's Technicolor wake as she heads to the car, feather blowing in the wind.

REFERENCES: *un arc-en-ciel* (m) = rainbow; *l'arrosage* (m) = watering; *très jolie* = very pretty; *le carnaval* (m) = carnival (a yearly celebration at school); *mais, il fait froid dehors!* = but it's cold outside!; *les échecs* (m) = chess; *d'accord?* = OK?; *la petite-fille* (f) = granddaughter; *les espadrilles* (f) = canvas shoes with cord soles

204 · · · · · · · · · · · · · · · · · · · · · · ·

Expressions

se mettre dans les plumes = to hit the sack
perdre ses plumes = to lose one's hair
vivre de sa plume = to live by one's pen, to be a writer by
    profession
voler dans les plumes à quelqu'un = to attack or criticize
    someone

Poignée

(pwan-yay)

noun, feminine

handful

The clouds have snuck in, bringing with them a *poignée* of neighborhood kids who remain holed up at our house.

Max has offered each of his friends one of those little square juice cartons marked *"pur jus de raisin"*; the box comes with a miniature straw to punch through a sealed hole in the top. I stab the *paille* into my own juice box and keep an eye on the *garçons* from the kitchen table, where I'm working.

The boys eat butter cookies and chocolate-filled wafers until, out of desperation (and out of *gâteaux*), they begin eating *pommes*. They circulate in and out of the kitchen with their quenchless thirst and bottomless bellies.

"Ne rentrez plus dans la cuisine!" I say, hiding the last can of soda in the vegetable crisper and sliding a few cookies behind the *machine à café*.

The four boys, aged nine to thirteen, lounge across the *canapé* and watch a *match de foot*. They can't seem to sit still, but move from couch to floor and back again.

Suddenly they're up and scrambling for the front door.

"What are you doing now?" I ask.

"Il ne pleut plus!"

Oh, it's stopped raining. I had not noticed.

Not only are they able to watch TV, *gigoter*, slurp, and eat, but they have one eye on the weather. No sooner has the last raindrop hit dirt than they're headed back out to the *terrain de foot* to kick the ball.

Out in the yard, the *footballeurs* wear their colorful *maillots* representing Barcelona, Real Madrid, and La France. When the weather takes another turn, I rush in to batten down the hatches before four hungry boys storm into the kitchen.

REFERENCES: *une poignée* (f) = handful; *un pur jus de raisin* (m) = pure grape juice; *une paille* (f) = (drinking) straw; *un garçon* (m) = boy; *le gâteau (sec)* (m) = cookie; *ne rentrez plus dans la cuisine!* = don't come back into the kitchen!; *une machine à café* (f) = coffee machine; *un match de foot* (m) = soccer game; *il ne pleut plus!* = it's no longer raining!; *gigoter* = fidget; *le terrain de foot* (m) = soccer field; *le footballeur (la footballeuse)* = soccer player; *le maillot* (m) = jersey (soccer)

Also

une poignée de porte = doorknob

Poisson

(pwa-sohn)

noun, masculine

fish

*F*ingers gliding over the *clavier*, I hardly noticed the sly look on my six-year-old's face as she entered the *bureau* and streamed past.

We share this office. I'm the writer, she's the artist; we each have our own work space and a dream, which suits us just fine. True, we are *serrées comme des sardines* at times, and she complains about my papers, which trail over to her space, and I complain about her crayons, which roll onto my desk. Otherwise we get along swimmingly.

"Hi, sweetie," I said.

"Salut, maman."

I kept typing as my daughter snuck around me, I believed, to cut to the next room. Instead she hovered at my back until my fingers froze and I turned around.

Ever so slight, I'd felt it, the punch of a dainty *demoiselle's* thumb. . . .

"What's up?"

"*Rien.*"

When your kid says nothing's up, something's fishy. As I turned, I heard the paper shift against the chair, and realized I'd been pinned with something.

Jackie stood, *muette comme une carpe,* before bursting out with laughter.

"*Poisson d'avril!*" she snickered.

I pulled the paper fish off my back. "*Haha! Trop drôle!*" I said, before admiring the rainbow of colors my daughter had *soigneusement* applied to the paper cutout.

"*Tu m'as eue!*"

208

Jackie was practicing on me before the big day. On April 1, the French partake in this harmless, if goofy, tradition: pinning or sticking a paper fish to the *dos* of an unsuspecting person.

Once again my freckle-faced colleague was there to bring a little splash of laughter and learning to the ebb and flow that is office life *à la campagne.*

REFERENCES: *un clavier* (m) = keyboard; *le bureau* (m) = office; *serrées comme des sardines* = squeezed in like sardines; *la demoiselle* (f) = young lady; *muet(te) comme une carpe* = tight-lipped, silent as a carp; *poisson d'avril* = April fool!; *trop drôle* = too funny; *soigneusement* = carefully; *tu m'as eue!* = you got me!; *le dos* (m) = back; *à la campagne* = in the country

Expressions

noyer le poisson = to drown the fish, to ruin a deal

être ni chair ni poisson = to be indecisive; to be neither fish nor fowl

être comme un poisson dans l'eau = to be in one's element

finir en queue de poisson = an unexpected, deceiving outcome

être comme un poisson hors de l'eau = to be like a fish out of water

Polir

(poh-leer)

to polish

The sign indicated thirteen kilometers to Figanières. When I shared that information with my seven-year-old copilot, she began to sing:

> *Un kilomètre à pied, ça use, ça use . . .*
> *Un kilomètre à pied, ça use les souliers!*
> *Deux kilomètres à pied, ça use, ça use . . .*
> *Deux kilomètres à pied, ça use les souliers!*
> *Trois kilomètres à pied, ça use, ça use . . .*

Several refrains later, we coasted into the quiet town and began looking for parking along the main street. I had come to this neighboring village on a mission—to capture its soul on film and, in the process, to explore and discover its beauty. I brought Jackie along for good luck and good company.

I saw an empty space and began to parallel-park. A street cleaner in a blue uniform scrubbed the sidewalk, stepping to the side, pausing here, ducking out there, in a tango with my *bagnole* as he tried not to get a toe caught under the tire of the microcar struggling into the macro *espace*.

"*Bonjour, monsieur,*" I said, stepping out of the car. "Are we allowed to park here?" I was somewhat impatient, wanting to get the parking chore over with so that I could begin collecting images.

Monsieur with the salt-and-pepper hair paused, putting the broom aside. "This is twenty-minute parking. If you're staying longer, you might want to park up the road. There is a bigger lot just past the town hall."

I thanked Monsieur and, as an afterthought, asked about the town's name. "It has nothing to do with figs, I imagine?"

"*Oh, non.*" He smiled. "*Voyons . . .*" He told me about the *fugue,* the fleeing of one group of settlers from another. "*Figanières* comes from *fuguer,* to run away." He seemed sorry that he couldn't add more detail to the story, and he bid Jackie and me farewell. "Just past the town hall and to your right," he added.

I noticed his eyes, as close to turquoise as eyes can be. He went back to scrubbing the brick *trottoir* with a broom, a pail of sudsy water to his side. He polished the floor of the village as a violinist might polish an instrument before a grand concert.

Jackie and I easily found parking at the suggested lot, and set out to find those colorful French-village wooden shutters, rock walls, and moss-covered stone fountains that continue to still my heart. Instead, we rounded each bend to find another dark, deserted courtyard. Looking up to the windowsills, I saw flowers dried in their pots, not a tumbling vine in sight.

It seemed every time we turned a corner, the man with the turquoise eyes was there, polishing the village floor. He didn't need to hum, his broom did that for him; there was joy in its sweep, gospel in its gait.

I stepped up my efforts to find that charming, still-elusive French scene. Like the sweeper, I scoured the streets for beauty, my eyes washing over the shadowy façades with their dull shutters and flowerless windowsills: winter in Provence.

"Come on, Jackie!" I said to my daughter, impatient to find something to capture the spirit of this sleepy village. We took the winding cobblestone stairs and marched up to the *église*. Instead of beauty I could see only how the light was not shining on the building as it should, as it would need to, in order for the photograph to be taken. "Nothing here," I said to Jackie. "Let's go!"

Back at the car I fumbled for the keys, which fell from my pocket, causing me to look down, past my *souliers*, to the polished brick path below. And that's when I noticed how clean the streets were. The sidewalk, made up of small red bricks arranged into rolling patterns, was spotless. Across the street, I saw the street sweeper. His dancing broom came to a halt upon the spiraling bricks, which were now flaming red from the sunlight. His turquoise eyes caught mine, and then, just then, I snapped the photo I wanted, if only in my mind. It was the one I had been chasing all afternoon, and it captured the essence, the beauty, grace, and spirit of this sleepy village in one neat scene. It had been everywhere, and around every corner. I had just been too out of focus to see it.

REFERENCES: *un kilomètre* . . . = one kilometer on foot, it wears, it wears . . . it wears down the shoes; *un espace* (m) = space; *voyons* = let's see; *la fugue* (f) = running away

Portefeuille

(port-uh-fuhy)

noun, masculine

wallet

From my window I watched our Citroën eclipse the iron gates and hang a left past the fading lavender patch. The vehicle rolled forward until its back fender lined up with the front door of our house, at which point the motor shut off.

Jean-Marc was home with the groceries. Food! Excited though I was, I decided to let him empty the trunk and put away the goods; after all, that *is* part of our new deal, I like to think, in which he does the grocery shopping while I work more at my desk, while keeping up my end of the housework. I'd already made the beds, hung out one load of laundry to dry, and folded another. I let a good fifteen minutes pass before retrieving the laundry basket and heading to the kitchen to greet my husband—careful to appear as industrious as he.

"How much did you spend?" said I, out of breath.

"*Cent soixante euros,*" said he, drying his brow with his shirt-sleeve.

With that I set down the laundry basket and went to open the fridge and visualize so many colorful *billets* metamorphosed into food form.

A cool blanket of air covered me from shoulders to ankles, then from forehead to knees as I knelt before the perishables. I counted two dozen single-serving tubs of yogurt, two small disks of Saint-Marcellin cheese, two packages of Emmental *râpé*, two family-sized loaves of whole wheat bread, two jars of *confiture*, and two tubs of tabbouleh. There must have been a *deux-pour-un* special at the supermarket. So far, I gave him credit for his food choices. Still, 160 euros—*for just this*? That's when I remembered the *congélateur*. . . .

I stood up to pull open the freezer door, only to find two boxed pizzas and two cartons of miniature ice-cream cones. *Cent soixante euros* . . . *Ouf!* I remembered the cupboards. . . .

On the shelves above the *four* I noted two boxes of pasta and two plastic containers of chocolate powder. There seemed to be a lot of food cloning going on in our kitchen, what with two of this and a double of that. My eyes darted over to my chocolate bar stash where I did *not* find two foil-wrapped replacements. I did see linguine linguine, cornflakes cornflakes, and *thon thon* (the latter next to the sardines sardines and *crevettes crevettes*).

Would that this were stocking for a rainy day. *Mais, non!* In the absence of other, more exotic (read: expensive) edibles (OK, this is the real reason why I no longer shop), we will be eating piles of pasta, tons of tabbouleh, and a sea of sardines this week. I closed the cupboard in defeat.

Now, if I could just get my husband's *portefeuille* to clone a few more euros so I can send him back to the store for the chocolate bar chocolate bar.

REFERENCES: *cent soixante euros* = 160 euros; *le billet* (m) = banknote; *râpé* = grated; *deux-pour-un* = two-for-one; *le congélateur* (m) = freezer; *le four* (m) = oven; *le thon* (m) = tuna; *la crevette* (f) = shrimp; *mais, non!* = absolutely not!

Expressions

avoir un portefeuille bien garni = to be well-off

mettre la main au portefeuille = to fork out (money)

Poulet

(poo-lay)

noun, masculine

chicken

Cotignac is a quiet French village located forty-five minutes west of the Var's capital, *c'est-à-dire*, Draguignan. The town's proximity to my village made it an ideal day trip for my aunt and uncle, in for a short but *sucré* visit from San Francisco.

The name Cotignac comes from the Latin *cotoneum* (*coing* in French) and means, of all things, "quince jam." We were not headed to this typical Provençal village for the *confiture* but to see the tufa.

"What is a tufa?" my aunt and I say, in unison. My uncle is sitting in the backseat, reading aloud on Cotignac. "Tufa is a kind of porous rock," my uncle begins . . .

"Oh, these roads are quite sinewy," my aunt says, clutching her seat. With that, I slow down and try to concentrate on the road, which is hard to do with so much gorgeous *paysage* filing by (and with the oohing and aahing of my passengers). This part of Provence is classified *zone verte,* meaning "green zone," as it is a protected area.

Cotignac is well known for its *falaise de tuf,* a *falaise* being a cliff. One half kilometer outside the village, my aunt wonders how the town will be situated. Just then we round the last bend and three breaths exhale, "Whoa!" The entrance is awe-inspiring, with the village in the forefront and the volcanic cliffs towering behind.

We pull into the *centre-ville* on a Monday morning and easily find parking in an *impasse,* not far from the tourist office.

"This town has nothing on yours," my uncle says. But the old shutters and shop fronts with their sometimes fading, sometimes colorful façades seem even more charming.

We take the narrow path up to the *mairie* and leave my uncle to wander back to the cliff. Apparently there are old olive presses at the base of the *falaise,* and caves, or *grottes,* inside. The town is a bit *morte* on a Monday morning and most of the shops are closed. No matter, viewing the old façades is enjoyable enough.

After the *balade* we stop for lunch at a corner café just next to the main fountain. On the outdoor blackboard menu, *"Blan-quette de veau . . . 9 euros"* is scribbled in white chalk. When the owner appears we ask her if there is chicken. In a whiskeyed voice she responds: *"Poulet?* Where do you see *poulet* on the menu?" She is visibly irritated and takes our menu.

"Non. Pas de poulet!" she confirms. We quickly order two Niçoise salads and the *plat du jour* in hopes of unruffling her feathers and clearing the air for a more relaxing atmosphere.

I am worried about what lunch will be like, and hope the woman's moodiness won't somehow be reflected in the food. Moments later the *patronne* returns with three mouth-watering meals. The food is fresh and appetizing.

With the owner in a better mood and in hopes of getting to the *âme* of this village, I ask: "Can you describe Cotignac—in one word?"

She looks up with a smile and says: "*Rocher. Vin rosé! Conviviale.*"

Conviviale—now that's an interesting choice! I thought about asking her to elaborate on this point and wondered if she considered herself one among the friendly villagers. On second thought, I didn't want to push it. Not after the *poulet* episode.

REFERENCES: *c'est-à-dire* = that is to say; *sucré* = sweet; *le centre-ville* (m) = the town center; *une impasse* (f) = dead end; *la blanquette de veau* (f) = veal stew in white sauce; *le poulet* (m) = chicken; *le patron (la patronne)* = owner; *une âme* (f) = soul; *le vin rosé* (m) = rosé wine

Expression

mon (petit) poulet = my love, my pet

Prénom

(pray-non)

noun, masculine

first name

$\mathcal{I}$n the spring of 1994 I wobbled around Marseilles with a soon-to-be born *franco-américain*. The French are very *sympathiques* to *les femmes enceintes,* and so I enjoyed no lines at the supermarket checkout and always found a seat on the crowded number 73 bus, which carried me to and from the *centre-ville* each day. All was bliss apart from the 'what-to-name-baby' dilemma. I wanted to call my son Evan but my husband objected; "The French will call him Heaven!" (And they wouldn't be incorrect, I think nowadays, as my son is divine!)

We settled on the *prénom* Maxime. The name might sound a bit feminine to an Anglophone, but it is a very masculine and somewhat common first name here in France. We call our son Max when we're in the States, just in case.

Though I never found the *prénom* Maxime feminine, I was

initially nonplussed by men who were *prénommés* Michel, Yves, Lilian, Janis, and Jacky. (My husband's uncle's name was even Yves-Marie!)

But then again I know quite a few women here who go by Fred and think nothing of it.

REFERENCES: *sympathique* = friendly, nice; *la femme enceinte* (f) = pregnant woman; *prénommé* = named; Fred, in this example, is short for Frédérique

Expression

se faire un prénom = to make a name for oneself

Pudibond

(pood-ee-bohn)

prim and proper

The first time I ever heard of Saint-Tropez was from an ad jingle that went like this: "Bain de Soleil for the Saint-Tropez tan." Thanks to that commercial I learned my first five French words and could pronounce them like a nine-year-old native.

In Saint-Trop (as the locals call it), Jean-Marc, Max, and I waddle across the beach. We are toting grass mats, plastic buckets, rakes, suntan lotion, magazines, fishing poles, flippers, and an eleven-month-old Jackie. We walk along the edge of the sea, where the *sable* is compact and easier to advance on.

"Ils sont là," Jean-Marc says, pointing to the group in the distance. Another fifty meters and we are nearly there; it is then that I hear the laughter. Ah, right, we must be a comical sight what with all the stuff we're dragging out with us . . . and so I chuckle along with the group.

As we approach, I realize they are not laughing at *us*. I look down to pale skin. I should have made time for a *bain de soleil* before vacation. Before long, I will learn that it isn't skin tone that sends the women into crying fits of laughter.

The *nanas* are lounging on the sand, their hair pulled back tight into sleek ponytails, with no makeup (no need), caramel tans, gold bracelets from Marseilles, and . . . half of their bathing suits missing. The top half, that is.

I pull my towel up and tuck the corner in before advancing any farther. *La honte*. Wearing full makeup and a swimsuit appropriate for deep-sea diving, I am a direct contrast to their bare busts and bronzed skin.

One of the sun goddesses stubs out her cigarette, stands up, and approaches me. *"Salut,"* she says. Just then I catch a glimpse of myself in the Frenchwoman's sunglasses. What I see: the subject, in the foreground, wearing a one-piece bathing suit; beyond, a beach full of *torses nus*.

Next, she taps on my collarbone, which is covered by Lycra from my one-piece suit. "This has got to go!" she says, in so many French words.

I remain miserable until I can finally reach a store, where I snap up the first two-piece I can find, a horrible combo in lime green.

At a beach near Fréjus, five years later . . .

I drape my towel over the chaise longue, adjusting my swimsuit (a present from Jean-Marc for Mother's Day). I am prepared this time around: tan, two-pieced, a featherlight touch of mascara, and sense of humor intact.

I notice something strange: the women aren't removing their tops, and their bellies are—a bit paunchy.

"*De toute façon*," one of the Frenchwomen begins, "it's not *la mode* anymore to go topless."

"That's right," another woman says, exhaling cigarette smoke and adding, "not very flattering either!"

I am momentarily confused. And then a strange compulsion visits me. I reach around to my back and pull at the string, quickly flipping over onto my stomach. I lie there facing the sand, a grin on my face, feeling very one up on the Frenchwomen in my own peculiar way.

REFERENCES: *le sable* (m) = sand; *ils sont là* = they are there; *un bain de soleil* (m) = sunbath, sunbathing; *la nana* (f) = girl; *la honte* (f) = shame, disgrace; *les torses nus* (m) = bare busts; *de toute façon* = in any case; *la mode* (f) = style

224

Also

la pudibonderie (f) = prudishness, primness

Raccourci

(ra-kor-see)

noun, masculine

shortcut

This weekend, thanks to Jackie and Max, I discovered new stomping grounds.

Our trio was headed to the village, *à pied*, to buy baguettes when Max casually mentioned a *raccourci*. I'm terrified to cut through other people's property, always taking the heavily treaded, most obvious public paths, but to please my son, I turned trailblazer.

Prefacing each turn with "Are you guys *sure* this is public?" I fretted my way forward.

The newly discovered path led to an old cascade that fell from a three-meter-tall ancient wheel. After slipping behind the eighteenth-century *bastide* to access the path (and taking advantage of the angle to peep inside the gate), we practically slid down the hill through the mud.

"Look at that, Mom," Jackie said, *mi-chemin,* pointing muddy fingers to the panoramic view of the village below, making me wonder why we don't go wandering more often.

REFERENCE: *mi-chemin* = midpath

Rallonge

(ra-lonzh)

noun, feminine

extension cord

*I*n France, a mother who fusses over her children is called *une maman poule,* a mother hen. In our home, we happen to have a *papa poule.* . . .

When Max and Jackie asked to sleep out, Jean-Marc prepared the tent for the three of them. I knew something was up when I saw the long *rallonge* trailing from the house, over the terrace, through the *pétanque* court, around the magnolia tree, and across the yard to the small two-man tent.

My husband explained that he had installed a fan and dispersed mosquito repellent throughout the tent. I noticed he had added two thick foam mattresses and had carefully tucked two feather pillows into the satiny sleeping bags. I half expected to find the sleeping bag tops turned back and a small square of foil-wrapped chocolate upon each pillow.

As nice as the accommodations were, I still felt uneasy about letting the kids use the fan.

"I don't feel comfortable with electricity trailing into the tent!" I said. Jean-Marc tensed. "It gets hot in there at night."

"People all over the world are sleeping in tents tonight, *sans électricité!* If the kids are going to rough it, then let them rough it! What's the point of sleeping out in a tent if you're going to have air artificially whirled in?"

(*À vrai dire*—truth be told—I wasn't really worried about spoiling the kids, but about safety. What if some freak storm rushed in and dampened the fan's cord?)

Jean-Marc looked resigned and for a moment I tried to relax and remember the adventure of sleeping out as a kid. I thought back to when my mom put up a two-man tent for my sister and me in our backyard. Though we didn't have an electric fan, Mom supplied us with a portable flashlight and a generous supply of Pop Rocks.

The electric fan issue resolved (by the agreement that there'd be no air whirled in artificially), I began to worry about how Jean-Marc would fit into the cramped space that remained to the side of the kids' mattresses. That's when I volunteered to sleep out, in the place of my husband.

Later, Jean-Marc came back out of the house with a blanket and more pillows. "You'll need these," he said, doing some last-minute fussing. He'd already added a lawn chair pad, which just filled what space remained, next to the kids' deluxe accommodations.

Something about a tent makes late-night conversations that much more sublime. As Max, Jackie, and I spoke to one another, our conversation was buoyed by a pastiche of late-night sounds:

228

in the distance, beneath the village, the occasional train whirring by; the echoing laughter of the neighbors after a late-night meal on the terrace; a passing car with the summer hit "Dragostea Din Tei" by the Romanian group O-Zone booming from its speakers. Only one thing missing: the *grenouilles*. Where were the frogs?

Later that night the cool air drugged us until we were almost asleep. I heard the creaking of the neighbor's wooden shutters as the woman drew them to a close, carefully fastening the metal bar into the clasp. The only remaining sound: the song of the cricket.

The next morning I awoke to the cry of a magpie. Then came the doves and, gradually, a symphony of half a dozen other birds I cannot name.

While we did not need the fan—in fact, the two kids migrated from their sleeping bags to underneath my blanket—I have Papa Poule to thank for the mosquito repellent: not a bite.

229

REFERENCE: *la grenouille* (f) = frog

Also

une table à rallonge(s) = an extendable table

une rallonge d'argent = some extra money

une histoire à rallonge = a never-ending story

un nom à rallonge = a long, complicated surname; a double-barreled name

Ramasser

(ra-ma-say)

to pick up

On Sunday, villagers owning even a square foot of French dirt were giddily tending to it for the first time this year. Whether out on their terraces or in their gardens, *sécateurs* in hand or rakes under arm, the *Arcois* were actively contemplating spring.

Jean-Marc and I left our garden for a leisurely stroll through the *voisinage*. The quiet outing turned into a veritable *chasse aux déchets*, or garbage hunt, when my husband found a wet plastic supermarket bag *par terre*. He picked up the bag and shook off the water, popping the impromptu container open with a swoop and a gust of air.

For the next two hundred or so meters Jean-Marc tended to the neighborhood litter, plucking up *mégots*, raking in gum wrappers, digging out a can of Kronenbourg here, a plastic cap there. I thought about how his homemade sea-urchin-catching mop-spear would have come in handy.

As we encountered other neighbors out on a walk, I found myself skipping a few steps ahead of *Monsieur Propre* and began to realize, not without guilt, that I was a little bit embarrassed by his behavior. We looked like Mr. and Mrs. Goody Two-shoes, a bit holier than thou, snapping up garbage on a fine *dimanche après-midi*.

Approaching another neighbor, Jean-Marc lunged forward, swiping up a bundle of pink toilet paper. I winced and said *"Bonjour"* to the man, unsure about which point I was more pressed to get across: that the *PQ,* or the *PQ* lunger, was *not* related to me.

Self-obsessive thoughts aside, seeing all that litter makes one wonder: if the discarded items were paper euro bills or unscratched lottery tickets, would they have so easily slipped from the hands of the original owner? While littering may be thoughtless, it's not accidental.

231

The bag now held six crushed cigarette packs, an empty yogurt container, a *prospectus,* a wad of pink toilet paper, dozens of *mégots,* gum and candy wrappers *à gogo,* three *canettes,* and a plastic water bottle.

By the time we arrived back at our house the plastic bag was three quarters full. *"Et voilà,"* Jean-Marc said, opening the *poubelle,* about to pitch the bag. Just then I glimpsed the lettering on the side of the sack, which read: *"Ne pas jeter dans la nature"*—do not litter.

We returned to our yard and Jean-Marc made a beeline to the shed, intent on organizing the garden *outils.* I wondered if, mixed in with the rakes, shovels, and other gardening paraphernalia, somewhere among the insect-repelling granules and various pest sprays, he had a bioorganic solution for litterbugs.

REFERENCES: *le sécateur* (m) = clippers; *un Arcois (une Arcoise)* = one who is from Les Arcs; *par terre* = on the ground; *le mégot* (m) = cigarette butt; *Monsieur Propre* = Mr. Clean; *le PQ* (slang) (m) = toilet paper; *le prospectus* (m) = leaflet; *à gogo* = galore; *la canette* (f) = can (of soda, beer); *un outil* (m) = tool

Expressions

ramasser quelque chose à la pelle = to obtain loads of something

être à ramasser à la petite cuillère = to be exhausted

ramasser une bûche/une gamelle/une pelle = to fall, to fall flat on one's face

Rang

(rahng)

noun, masculine

row

Sunday found Max, Jackie, Jean-Marc, and me in the northernmost part of Provence, in a quaint papal town between Avignon and Orange.

"*C'est le château* tout *nouveau du pape!*" said Max, trying to make sense of the village's name. "That's right, Max. Châteauneuf-du-Pape—the brand-new home of the pope," his father added.

Or *papes,* for it was the French popes of Avignon that used the castle, residing in the fourteenth-century version of this charming vintners' village back when Pope John XXII was in charge. I looked from the château to the parcel of land before us, where dozens of *rangs* of vines were weighed down by fat red grapes. After a very bumpy ride from the *galet*-packed dirt road, we had arrived at Vaudieu, one of the four parcels of land belonging to Jean-Marc's uncle.

I loved the name Vaudieu and wondered what it meant. Jean-Marc wasn't able to tell me, and I forgot to ask his uncle. I couldn't help but want it to mean "worthy of God." The *vau* part sounds like *vaut* from the verb *valoir* (to be worth) and *dieu* is French for God. Certainly the fertile ground beneath us, known for producing the famous *treize cépages*—thirteen of the most sought-after grape varieties in France—could be said to be "worthy of God"!

At the end of several *rangs* of vines, around two dozen other *vendangeurs*—a mix of family and friends of Jean-Marc's uncle Jean-Claude—were already busy picking grapes. Each year it is *les retrouvailles*, as we reunite with people that we will see only while picking grapes at Châteauneuf-du-Pape. Our common goal is to help the winemaker, and we are happy to return home with a few bottled souvenirs, and memories of a day in the vines. *"Bonjour! Salut! Comment ça va?"* the *vendangeurs* said, welcoming us (and the extra helping hands), but we were careful not to stop to exchange kisses and further delay the *vendange*.

Equipped with *sécateurs, seaux,* and medical examiner's gloves, we each selected a *rang* and began picking the *grenache* and *clairette* grapes.

At the Vaudieu parcel, the vines are low and *en gobelet*, free-standing and not attached to wire. Jean-Claude tells me that the word *gobelet* reflects the vine's shape, which slumps into a goblet form when it is not fastened up along a wire. I always think of these vines as being the hardest ones to harvest because they seem lower to the ground. Later that afternoon I would learn that vines *en palissage* (trained along a wire fence) were just as grueling to pick, as they sometimes wind around the wires that hold them up, making it difficult to see just where the base of the grape bunch is in order to clip it.

Châteauneuf-du-Pape, my husband tells me, is a favored grape-growing location for its proximity to the Rhône, its smooth, round *galets,* which soak in the Provençal sun and warm the vines, and the famous mistral wind, which keeps the grapes dry and *sain* (relatively free from the *pourriture*).

After only two hours of picking, we stopped for a three-hour lunch. First we had a peek in the hangar, where the fruits of our labor were already being processed. Into the *fouloir* the grapes went. The skins were gently cracked before being vacuumed up into the *cuve* via a six-inch-wide hose. Once in the *cuve,* the grapes began to macerate, the juice taking on the color of the skins. The sugar level was measured at 13, which reflects the alcohol content at 13 percent, a bit low for a Châteauneuf-du-Pape wine (last year's *récolte* was around 14.5).

After a lunch of homemade ratatouille, ham quiche, and *porc à la moutarde,* we learned the good news: there would be only three more *rangs* to harvest! We headed out to the Syrah grapes, light on our toes, the only American in our group whistling "O Happy Day."

Six twisted and sticky *rangs* later my whistle ran dry and I realized that the little white three-*rang* lie was just what the *chef d'équipe* needed to lure us from the never-ending *repas* and back out to the *rangs.*

REFERENCES: *le pape* (m) = pope; *un galet* (m) = a pebble; *le vendangeur (la vendangeuse)* = grape picker; *les retrouvailles* (f, pl) = reunion; *un seau*

(m) = pail, bucket; *sain* = healthy; *la pourriture* (f) = rot; *le fouloir* (m) = grape crusher; *une cuve* (f) = tank; *la récolte* (f) = harvest; *le chef d'équipe* = man in charge of the workers

Also

un rang de perles = a string or rope of pearls
deux (trois, quatre . . .) jours de rang = two (three, four . . .) days in a row

Expressions

en rangs serrés = in close order
de premier rang = first class, first rate
de haut rang = noble, of high rank
du plus haut rang = of highest standing
formez vos rangs! = fall in!
par rang d'âge/de taille = in order of age, of size
le rang social = social status
rompre les rangs = to break ranks, to fall out
se mettre sur un rang = to get in line
serrer les rangs = to close ranks, to close up
sortir du rang = to rise from the ranks
se mettre sur les rangs = to come forward as a candidate

Rebonjour
(ruh-boh-zhoor)
hello again

The French have a popular phrase: *"C'est simple comme bonjour"*—it's as easy as hello (or to mention an English equivalent: it's as easy as ABC). How ironic, then, that greeting someone can be *difficile comme adieu,* or as hard as saying good-bye.

In France, if you want to seem even more odd to the French, just say "Hello" one time too many. Les Français don't understand the Anglophone affinity for repeating "Hello" at another point in a twenty-four-hour time frame. The French say *"Bonjour"* once—*point final.*

That said, the Frenchies have come up with a way to regreet one another, using the ultrapopular term *rebonjour.* But after twelve years in this country, I continue to make the repeat-greet *faux pas.*

At fourteen o'clock, after a two-hour lunch break, a colleague returns to the office where I work.

"*Bonjour*, Fifi!" I say.

Our *caviste* looks at me perplexed (by now I'm used to this reaction, so I'm still not sure what's up).

"But . . . haven't we seen each other already?" he says, pushing a cheek forward to accept my greeting, only I don't kiss him this time.

"Oh yeah, that's right," I say, wondering just how thick my head must be that it can't absorb French etiquette rule 3,027-b after all this time.

"*Rebonjour, alors!*"—hello again, then!—he says, content to put the matter straight.

Fifi returns to the cellar to glue the *étiquettes* on the bottles of wine. In the meantime, I fuss over my own vintage selection of French greetings, carefully adding a label to my most recent three-syllabled acquisition: *rebonjour*.

REFERENCES: *le point final* (m) = period; fourteen o'clock = 2 PM (the French use the twenty-four-hour clock); *le caviste* (m) = person who works in a cellar; Fifi = a shortened version of Philippe; *une étiquette* (f) = label

Réveiller

(ray-vehyay)

to wake up

From the window above my desk, I saw the two women approach our gate. In the time it took *les dames* to find the *sonnette*, I tried to hide, but Jackie sacked that plan by running to the door to greet the strangers.

The women were dressed in crisp cotton dresses and wore inviting smiles. One of the two solicitors patted a bun of gray hair, verifying her neat appearance.

"Bonjour, madame!" one of the ladies said, handing me a slim magazine. The cover depicted a woman sneezing, so I figured it was a health journal.

"Do you want me to *abonner*?" I said, adding, "I don't speak French very well."

"Ah—we may have one in German," the other lady answered, flipping through her purse.

"I don't speak German either," I said, hoping to seal a "no deal."

"Ce n'est pas grave," the women said in unison, preparing to leave.

"Don't you want this back?" I said, clutching the magazine.

"Non, madame. We'll be back next week. See you then. *Au revoir!"* And with that the ladies turned and disappeared down the path.

Before I knew what hit me, the door-to-door divas were gone, having secured another rendezvous. I was at once baffled and impressed by their savoir faire.

I returned to my desk, gift in hand. *Réveillez-Vous* the magazine's title read. I flipped past the sneezing lady when a second booklet fell to the floor, its title: *Le Tour de Garde Annonce Royaume de Jéhovah.*

240   REFERENCES: *la sonnette* (f) = bell; *abonner* = to subscribe; *ce n'est pas grave* = don't worry about it; *réveillez-vous* = *wake up*

· · · · · · · · · · · · ❀ · · · · · · · · · · · ·

Expressions

être réveillé en sursaut = to be woken up with a start
réveiller les consciences = to awaken people's consciences

· ·

Rideau

(re-doh)

noun, masculine

curtain

Les Arcois stood outside the theater dressed in their Sunday best on a Saturday afternoon. Entrance was *gratuit* and the seats limited. When the doors opened, we crowded into the auditorium.

"*Il y a quelqu'un là?*" I said, pointing to a single seat in the middle of the second row.

"*Allez-y, madame.*"

With that, I sat down.

The choreographer shouted "*Rideau!*" and the curtain came up.

The dancers stood onstage, some pulling at their underwear, some wiping their noses, some shielding their eyes from the bright lights. Their faces sparkled from *paillettes,* and their round tummies remained in a carefree paunch.

I searched in vain for my favorite dancer, looking for a mop of blond hair in a sea of *têtes foncées.*

A man seated in the row behind me chatted nonstop. The words *"Fermez-la!"* pushed at my lips, but I bridled my mouth and focused my attention on finding *her*.

Many of the dances were choreographed to American rap music, and I sat cringing at the vulgar words and double entendres, finding little relief in the fact that the dancers and most of the audience did not speak English.

When the choreographer shouted *"Rideau!"* for the fourth time, the black velvet curtain rose again.

There—she—was.

My eyes stung and glossed over the instant she came into view. She had on a black leotard with one white pant leg fashioned over her left *jambe*. (Half of the girls wore white skirts over their tights, half one baggy pant leg.) As she leaped and twirled across the stage my body jolted forward, but I held my arms back. Would she trip? Would she fall?

Despite my *angoisse,* Jackie's face was relaxed, and she seemed *confiante.* Only six months ago, at another dance performance, she concentrated on the dancers to her left and to her right, following their every move. Not this time.

"J'ai bien répété"—I practiced a lot—she would tell me later, in the car ride home. *"Je me suis bien concentrée"*—I really concentrated.

"Plus on grandit, plus on a peur"—the bigger we get, the more afraid we are—the choreographer had said before introducing the last group of dancers, who came after Jackie, adding that they had *le trac,* or stage fright.

At seven, Jackie is still too young to worry and fret about

what could go wrong; whether onstage before an audience of teary-eyed *mamans* and *papas* or beyond the Great Curtain that is life, where teary-eyed takes on another meaning.

For now (and forever) I'll worry and fret for her. *C'est normal, car je suis plus grande.*

REFERENCES: *gratuit* = free; *il y a quelqu'un là?* = is someone (sitting) there?; *allez-y* = go ahead; *les paillettes* (f) = sequins (here, sparkly powder); *la tête foncée* = dark head; *fermez-la* = close it (= be quiet); *la jambe* (f) = leg; *l'angoisse* (f) = anxiety; *confiant(e)* = confident; *plus on grandit, plus on a peur* = the bigger we get, the more afraid we are; *c'est normal, car je suis plus grande* = it's normal, as I am bigger

243

Expressions

tirer les rideaux = to draw or close the curtains

grimper aux rideaux = to climb the curtains, to be very excited

tirer le rideau sur quelque chose = to cease to talk about a subject

tomber en rideau = to break down (in car)

un rideau de fumée = a smoke curtain

un rideau de feu = a sheet of fire

Rouspéter

(roos-pay-tay)

to grumble

Max and Jackie are becoming veritable *rouspéteurs,* probably due to the approach of winter break. By the time a school vacation arrives, my six- and eight-year-olds are worn out from the learning grind.

In France, most grade school children attend school from 8:30 AM to 4:30 PM—including Saturday in our district! As if that weren't enough of a day, once home, children as young as six years old are in for homework.

My kids' teachers suggest that *le devoir* last only fifteen minutes. Max must learn and recite aloud one new poem per week and six-year-old Jackie is already required to note down her homework assignment (in cursive!) in a daily journal.

Jackie was ill all last week and so missed school. This morning she inquired, "Do I need to go to school?" When I replied, *"Oui!"* she began to fret about exams.

The Wednesdays-off-but-school-on-Saturdays plan is disorienting for an American mom, to say the least, but mostly it's downright unaccommodating. Going away for the weekend is out of the question, and for those who work outside the home, Wednesday poses a scheduling *souci* in which it becomes necessary to find a day-care solution. But the French are used to that as the children are on some sort of school break every five weeks! Nothing to grumble about there—if you're a kid, that is.

When I ask Jean-Marc what the French reasoning is behind no-school Wednesdays, he tells me it represents a midweek break for the kids. But homework on a Friday night—which remains as foreign a concept to me as the language once was—sure seems like a steep price to pay!

REFERENCES: *un rouspéteur (une rouspéteuse)* = moaner; *le devoir* (m) = homework; *le souci* (m) = worry

245

Expression

se faire rouspéter par quelqu'un = to be chewed out by
   someone

Sapin de Noël

(sa-pan duh no-el)

nouns, masculine

Christmas tree

On Saturday Jean-Marc, Max, and Jackie headed off to the supermarket parking lot to select this year's *sapin de Noël*. When Jean-Marc's Renault rolled into our driveway, I knew from the look of things (no branches sticking out of any collapsible part of the car) that this year's tree would be similar to last year's: *minuscule*.

Gone are my American Christmases. The ten-foot spruce my mom managed to drag in and install each year will not be mimicked in my *salon* this season. But the "Christmas tree thing" is one issue I have gotten over. When I realized how hard it was to find a whopping spruce for sale in my neck of the French woods, and what price such a tree would cost, if found, I let it go. But I still miss that pungent, fresh pine scent that *sapins* don't seem to have over here in France.

Integration has a funny way of creeping up on you, as witnessed in my change of heart last year, when I finally came under the charm of the *petit sapin*. I must admit that it has come as a relief to no longer pine over the Christmas tree *d'antan* and, instead, to merrily spruce up our own little evergreen.

With a new attitude intact, I approached the Renault to unload our tree, and as I flipped open the trunk, the spirit of the season took hold.

REFERENCE: *d'antan* = of yesteryear

Soif

(swaf)

noun, feminine

thirst

At the El Dorado Cinema in Draguignan I paid 18 euros for three theater seats. The *guichetière* slid the *billets* beneath the *vitrine* and I collected them before advancing to the popcorn stand: one of those old-fashioned glass boxes filled halfway up with puffed white kernels. A Frenchwoman, hidden behind the puffed mass, filled paper cups with the sugary snack. Once again, I yearned for buttery, salted popcorn, something I've yet to see in any French movie theater.

I noticed for the first time a stack of blue plastic sleds and wondered just what *sleds* were doing at a movie theater. But before I could strain my delicate *cerveau* farther, Max, Jackie, and their friend Baptiste selected a sled, and that is when I saw that the metal blades were missing. Just then the French lady behind me instructed her son to grab a booster seat. Aha.

"Tenez," said the girl behind the popcorn machine, handing over the cups. We took them and made our way into the vintage theater. The five of us installed ourselves: three on the booster seats, two *sans siège bleu*. The theater seats being sunk in, it was necessary for the bigger kids to use the booster chairs as well.

"Oh, les pipelets! Taisez-vous!" Brigitte said. The boys, who sat next to her, were chatting away like, well, girls. When their word mills weren't turning their bodies were twisting, fidgeting, and seesawing.

"That's OK, they'll calm down when the movie starts," Brigitte reassured me.

When the *pipelets* piped down, we settled in with anticipation to watch the latest Pixar flick: *Les Indestructibles*. I was delighted when the lights came down and peace permeated the cozy theater. If only for a nanosecond.

"J'ai soif!" Jackie began.

"Quit eating that popcorn, then. It's making you thirsty!"

I wasn't exactly sure if sugared popcorn had the same thirst-creating effect as the salty kind, but I wasn't going to take the chance.

After three or four *soif* pleas, I became concerned that the other moviegoers would put their sweet popcorn aside, pull out their portable phones, and dial *Allô Enfance Maltraitée*.

Out of *politesse*, I asked the others if I could get them something to drink.

"T'as soif, Brigitte?"

"Non, merci."

"T'as soif, Baptiste?"

"Non, merci."

"T'as soif, Maxime? Tu veux boire?"

"Oui!"

Humph!

Jackie and I made our way through the *obscurité* out to the reception, to the vending machines. Theaters in our area are very low-maintenance, and drinks and snacks—apart from the sugary popcorn—are purchased from coin-operated machines.

Two pieces of paper were taped to the vending machine: one read *"2 Euros,"* the other, *"En Panne."*

We returned to our seats, *sans boissons*. I figured Jackie would leave me in peace, now that she was convinced that there were no sugary drinks to slurp. I made myself cozy, adjusted my glasses, and heaved a sigh of relief. Back to *le film!*

"J'ai soif!" came the little voice beside me.

The next time an animated picture passes through town, I just might leave the chatterboxes and *ah-swa-fay* home.

REFERENCES: *le guichetier (la guichetière)* = ticket counter clerk; *un billet* (m) = ticket; *une vitrine* (f) = window; *tenez (tenir)* = here (take it); *le cerveau* (m) = brain; *un siège bleu* (m) = blue seat; *un pipelet* (m) = a chatterbox; *taisez-vous!* = quiet down!; word mill (from the French *un moulin à paroles*) = a chatterbox; *j'ai soif* = I'm thirsty; *Allô Enfance Maltraitée* = child abuse hotline; *la politesse* (f) = politeness; *t'as soif?* (informal) = are you thirsty?; *tu veux boire?* = do you want to drink (something)?; *l'obscurité* (f) = darkness; *en panne* = out of order; *une boisson* (f) = drink; *ah-swa-fay* (pronunciation for *assoiffés*) = the thirsty ones

Also

un soiffard (une soiffarde) = someone who likes to drink, one who drinks too much alcohol

Expressions

avoir soif = to be thirsty
jusqu'à plus soif = until one's thirst is quenched
garder une poire pour la soif = to keep a pear for the thirst, to put something aside for a rainy day

Sous-vêtement

(soo-vet-mahn)

noun, masculine

underwear

The difference between me and my neighbor down the road is in the items drying along our clotheslines.

Out pinning up laundry, and low on clothespins, I pile items one atop the other (one sock at each armpit of a shirt, a washcloth over a tea towel . . .).

When the linens are up, I reach for the undertoned underwear—the *culottes*, the *soutien-gorge*, my husband's *caleçons*—and hang them on the middle line, in between the sheets and the towels, which are on the first and third lines (taking care to camouflage the underthings from the man next door).

My neighbor's clothesline is a different story entirely. I marvel at how she places her lacy underwear up front and center, showcasing her she-things under the burning stage light that is the *soleil*. Her clothesline is located on a main road and her laundry is known to stop traffic. As you're driving by her frillies, minding your own business, a bright object flashes in your peripheral vision—that would be one of her gumball-colored bras—and it causes your head to slam right or left, depending on which direction you are traveling in.

As cha-cha-cha and vampy as her *étendoir* is, with its slink and its slank and the colorful bras *et compagnie* that hang out there, it has, nonetheless, a very classic undertone to it, with the oh-so-French dish towels, the checkered tablecloth, and her husband's classic Marcel undershirts. There is balance and order on her line. (Did you see those socks? One perfectly straightened sock per pin.)

I could learn a thing or *deux* from the neighbor down south, not the least of which how to hang a sock. If I stick around long enough, there may be a lesson in how hanging one's frillies up leads to letting one's hair down. Or vice versa.

REFERENCES: *le caleçon* (m) = boxer shorts; *un étendoir* (m) = clothesline; *et compagnie* = and the rest

Tache

(tash)

noun, feminine

spot

*J*ackie and I are building sandwiches. She didn't want the instant tabbouleh that I offered to whip together, so I've set out a selection of *jambon, tomates, fromage,* and *pain.* While her sandwich is rising into a pyramid, mine has taken on a saucer shape, much like the top of Seattle's Space Needle.

We settle in front of the *télé* to watch the *Midi les Zouzous* half-hour cartoon fest. In France there are fewer commercial breaks, but the *pubs* last longer—up to ten minutes. Apparently the public television stations (state-run, more funding) have fewer *pubs* than the private stations, which include a commercial break or two during films.

We are halfway through our sandwiches when a *pub* comes on in which a little French kid is cramming a melting candy bar into the pocket of his white *veste.* Jackie and I look at each other and wince. In the next scene, a little girl paints on clown-sized red lips with her mother's *rouge-à-lèvres*, then pops the extended tube into her pocket. Jackie and I gasp. Viewers are encouraged not to worry: product X will remove *taches de chocolat*, and also *taches de graisse, de pelouse,* and *taches de maquillage*.

"*Ils disent tout ça pour vendre!*" Jackie says. Perhaps it is true that they say all that to sell a product. From my six-year-old's reaction, I gather she must've been watching cartoons with her skeptical dad recently.

Another commercial comes on in which a woman places a strip of transparent paper over her front teeth. In the next scene she is smiling to her colleagues, teeth glimmering; it is *sous-entendu,* or understood, that the strip has removed the *taches de café, de thé,* and *de vin* (the coffee, tea, and wine stains) on her teeth. Just as I head for the kitchen to grab a pen and scrap of paper to note down the brand, Jackie sighs, "*N'importe quoi!*" (or as we say back home, "Hogwash!").

My kids are beginning to figure out that the promises they hear via the *pubs* don't always hold up. Max was particularly *déçu* recently when he bought a jar of name-brand gel and carefully pushed up the sides of his hair into a hard shark fin atop his head. Returning from school that day, he complained: "*Ça ne marche pas leur truc!*"—their trick doesn't work!—pointing to the collapsed hair. The *fin* had capsized, just like some of the claims on the *télé*.

Paper and pen in hand, full of pearly white wishes, I return to sit next to Jackie, who is still shaking her head in disbelief over the *pub* promises. As I record the name of the tooth whitener, I

255

remember Max's hair gel and realize that my kids have begun to see the light in the wake of flopped fins and the advertisements before them. Jackie and I finish our sandwiches while she doodles over the name-brand toothpaste on the paper, with the help of my pen.

REFERENCES: *la télé* (f) = TV; *le midi* (m) = noon; *une pub* (f) = commercial; *une veste* (f) = jacket; *le rouge-à-lèvres* (m) = lipstick; *le maquillage* = makeup; *déçu* = disappointed

Also

sans tache = spotless, unblemished
une tache d'huile = an oily mark, oil stain
une tache de graisse = a grease mark
une tache d'encre = an ink stain
une tache de vin = a wine stain, a strawberry mark on
   the skin
une tache de rousseur = a freckle
une tache de sang = a bloodstain

Expressions

faire tache = to stick out like a sore thumb
faire tache d'huile = to gain ground

Toquade

(tow-kahd)

noun, feminine

crush

$\mathcal{I}$ pad across the living room in my robe and slippers, making a beeline toward my son. Arms open wide, I gather him up and linger a few moments in his toothpaste-scented cloud.

"*Maman, arrête. Tu me décoiffes!*" This he mumbles, because he really wants the hug but he also really wants the cool hair.

"What's that?" I say, fully aware of what he has said.

"*Tu me décoiffes.*"

"I'm messing up your hair?"

He looks at the ground, kicks his left foot against the floor, and stifles a grin. He is in love and he has a helmet of gel on his head to prove it.

"Are you all gussied up for your girlfriend?" I say, thinking what a shame it is that he doesn't understand the same English that I understood at the age of nine—expressions like "gussied up." But he gets the gist.

"No!" he assures me, looking as repulsed as he can.

"Oh. Well, you look awfully *beau!*"

"Thanks, Mom," he says, kicking the other foot to the floor.

Max's latest *toquade* is cool for two reasons: she likes soccer and her initials happen to be the same as Max's favorite team, Olympique de Marseille—*OM.*

My French dictionary lists the noun *toquade* as meaning *"un goût vif et passager pour quelqu'un"* (a keen and fleeting taste for someone). That is enough to reassure this *maman—pour le moment.* If he shows too much interest in OM, I'll quit buying him the hair gel.

REFERENCES: *tu me décoiffes!* = you're messing up my hair!; *beau* = handsome; *pour le moment* = for the time being

258

＊

Expression

avoir une toquade pour quelqu'un = to have a crush on somebody

Transpirer

(trahn-spee-ray)

to sweat

Our plane flew into the "Valley of the Sun" when blackness covered the desert, roughly twenty-four hours after my voyage began. I settled in for a restless night of sleep on my sister's *canapé*.

In Phoenix, I would spend the next week readjusting to my native culture, running head-on into, and tripping over, the Frenchness that has grown on me, at times like a third foot. From etiquette to, well, sweat, the cultural crashes or situations that transpired were many.

La Politesse—Etiquette

It began with the automatic greetings I gave friends and new acquaintances: a kiss on each cheek instead of a hug—not a cultural gaffe per se, as Americans sometimes greet one another this way (just not the ones I grew up with!).

Le Langage—Language

What most Arizonans don't do is mouth *"Merci"* when another driver yields. Or say *"Voilà!"* when what they really meant was, "There you have it," or, "Here you are," or, "That's what happened."

Le Ménage—Housekeeping

After meals *chez ma soeur* I emptied the plates' contents into the garbage can. "This is America, and not the Middle Ages," my brother-in-law said, pointing to the sink. I had forgotten about garbage disposals. Not that they don't exist in France. I just haven't come across one yet.

When the clothes I'd hung out to dry disappeared, I had a word with the *beau-frère,* who mentioned something about neighborhood regulations, or "codes," and the fact that they had a perfectly operating dryer right in the house.

Le Transport—Transportation

Driving down Camelback Road, I gawk at cars the size of a quaint French *cabanon.* As we pull up to the stoplight at Sixty-eighth Street, I peer into one of the monster vehicles. A lone traveler, surrounded by a mass of empty-space-on-wheels, stares back.

260

Les Courses—Shopping

When I reach out to bag my own groceries, the bag boy is oddly amused by such novel shopper behavior. After that, he doesn't dare ask if he can help me out to the car.

Même la Transpiration—Even Sweat!

Standing in line at a department store to purchase a pair of socks, I noticed that the lady ahead of me was paying $18 for Donna Karan deodorant.

"Does it really work better than the other stuff?" I asked.

"Oh, it's wonderful! It has a great scent!"

"But does it beat perspiration?"

"It does."

261

I stared at the price tag. "How long does it last? I mean, the stick."

The clerk and the customer exchanged blank looks. Silence.

Just then the tip of my nose began to *transpirer*—my automatic reaction to awkward situations.

"Well," I said, "I guess it depends—doesn't it?—the stick life of deodorant . . . on whether you do a once-over"—here I paused to wave an invisible deodorant stick skyward—"or an up-'n'-down swipe . . . or up and down, up and down. I suppose a stick of deodorant could last anywhere from two months to six months, depending . . ."

The women seemed distracted by the thought, until one admitted, "When the stick gets low, I dig the rest out—it lasts longer that way."

"*Dig?* You have to *dig?*" I replied. "That's so—*Middle Ages!*"

REFERENCE: *chez ma soeur* = at my sister's

· · · · · · · · · · · · · ❧ · · · · · · · · · · · ·

Also

la transpiration (f) = perspiration, sweat

· ·

Trombone

(trawn-bon)

noun, masculine

paper clip

Kneeling before my seven-year-old, I reach up to fasten her coat. I pull the dangling *trombone* from my lip, bend out the end, and thread the paper clip through the hole where the zipper's original pull tab once hung. *Voilà!* An *astuce* I learned from the *assistante maternelle,* who, I imagine, has saved hundreds of *fermetures éclair* in her school days. (How is it that those zipper pull tabs disappear? The mass exodus of zipper pull tabs from our children's coats to—well, *that* is the question . . . to the Bermuda Zipper Triangle?—continues to perplex me.)

"Did you pack a *goûter?*" I ask my daughter, beginning my morning checklist/commentary, which includes: Do you have your *ticket de cantine?* Are you sure you can wear that thing in your hair to school? Are you allowed to bring *those?* Let's see your fingernails! Remind me to cut them tonight.

"It's *un goûter* and not *dégoûté*," Jackie says, in her usual "by the way" fashion; she offers plenty of these "by the way" tidbits in her quest to improve my French.

When my ears hear the sound *day*, my brain registers the French word *des*, as in *des goûters*, or more than one snack, and I am reminded that the children are to bring only one midmorning snack: "*Un fruit, par exemple,*" the *maîtresse* had suggested, and not *plusieurs*, otherwise the kids lose their appetite and don't eat all of their lunch.

Jackie's sentence, as I have heard it, is then: "It's *un goûter* and not *des goûters*"—one snack and not snacks—and it makes perfect sense that she has reminded me of this, as multiple snacks, packed by those militant *mamans poules*, are becoming a real issue at school.

264

"I know, I know," I say to my daughter, pulling up the new *trombone* zipper tab, satisfied with my last-minute repair.

"*Dégoûté, maman!*" Jackie repeats, and just then I realize I've been had. What I thought was a "by the way" tidbit was really another language snare, set by my now-snickering seven-year-old. Once again the joke is on me, only I'm not sure just what I've missed this time.

"*Dégoûté! blehhh! blehhh!*" Jackie teases.

"*Des goûters* . . . snacks," I whisper to myself, slowly. And again, "*Day-goo-tay.*" As I pronounce the word aloud this last time, I see it!—"disgusted"—which in French is the word *dégoûté*, and which sounds like *des goûters*, or snacks.

"Ah, *dégoûtés*. OK, gotcha—you little French word wizard!"

Blehhhh. Blehhh. Blehhh. When will I master this language?

Perhaps by the time they find all those missing zipper tabs, boats, and planes in the Bermuda (Zipper) Triangle.

REFERENCES: *une astuce* (f) = trick; *un(e) assistant(e) maternel(le)* = teacher's assistant (also child caregiver); *la fermeture éclair* (f) = zipper; *un ticket de cantine* = a lunch ticket; *dégoûté* = disgusted; *un fruit, par exemple* = fruit, for example; *la maîtresse* = teacher; *plusieurs* = several

Trousse

(troos)

noun, feminine

case

Max and Jackie accomplished several *aller-retours*, lugging sacks from the car, while I began storing the groceries.

My six- and eight-year-olds specialize in food retrieval, but also in food storage, so when the *coffre* was finally emptied, they gladly joined me in arranging the items.

I watched as they thoughtfully freed water bottles from tightly wrapped bundles, tubs of yogurt from flimsy cardboard packaging, and separated three-pack cans of green beans from industrial-strength plastic wrapping. I marveled at how they proceeded to store the items in a user-friendly way, unlike their *maman*, who throws such bundles into the *frigo*.

Handing Jackie a can of shaving cream, I said: "Would you please put this in Papa's sack?"

She looked at me quizzically.

"I mean, Papa's *bag*."

She stood silent.

"You know, the *machin* in the bathroom where his stuff is."

"You mean his *trousse de toilette*," she said, putting great emphasis on the last three words.

I'd like to think it was just on the tip of my tongue, that word. The truth is, it was stored in the far corner of my mind, like those old envelopes of dried soup that keep getting pushed to the back of the cupboard as the kids arrange the new dried goods on the front part of the shelf. What's important is that *trousse* is back up front and center in the language locker that is my mind. I'll see it next time I go looking for it, just like I'll find the new box of oatmeal tomorrow morning.

REFERENCE: *une trousse de toilette* = a toiletry case

267

Also

une trousse à outils = a tool kit

une trousse de maquillage = makeup bag

une trousse à pharmacie = a first-aid kit

une trousse de secours = a first-aid kit

Expression

aux trousses de = hot on the heels of

Vedette

(vuh-det)

noun, feminine

star

$\mathcal{I}$n Saint-Tropez the wind whipped through the narrow streets, chasing away tourists and making for a shivery welcome to those who held fast to the cobblestone paths. If most of the colorful wooden shutters weren't already latched, I'd have sworn it was the *mistral* that slapped them shut first.

I gave the woman in the pizza *camionnette* two coins totaling 4 euros. In return, she handed me two slices of pizza and grumbled when I asked if she would throw out the wrapper. *"Quel bon accueil!"*—what a nice welcome!—Jean-Marc said, careful to remain within earshot. We were eating *sur place,* so to speak, just across the gravel path from the pizza van. We took our lunch to the *banc* and sat down to marvel over the off-season.

Thirty miles inland, I have left our home, its chores, my office, and its paperwork behind, if only for a day. When Jean-

Marc invited me to go prospecting with him to find new accounts for his wine exporting business, I could not resist tagging along and taking in new sea-scented scenery.

At the last appointment, the shopkeeper explained that on a typical winter day like today, he is lucky to make 100 euros in wine sales, but that in high season (July and August), if he hasn't pulled in 15,000 euros by closing time, he's having a bad day.

From the *Place des Lices,* where the market was in full swing despite the season, we left the cold bench and took shelter in a famous café. I pushed open the glass door and was met by a thick embroidered curtain. When I parted the heavy drapes the atmosphere leaped forward. Nothing about the café was *ordinaire,* least of all the clientele.

Large oil canvases dressed the walls. There were four small tables on the enclosed terrace; around the tables, wide sunken chairs in soft caramel-colored leather. The clients were draped across the chairs, sipping red wine and pastis. Though the guests appeared hyperblasé, the minute the curtain parted and a new customer walked in, champagne flutes paused midair and all eyes shot up.

I made my way through the bar to the *petit coin.* At the foot of the stairs I saw the saloon-type doors and pushed them open to discover a tiny room with a long, horizontal steel tray tilted against the wall. A toilet apparatus for men? I backed out and climbed the stairs; at the top, a card table with a woman sitting behind it. The basket before her held an array of cigarettes. When I reached down to find my pockets missing, she said, "*Allez-y,*" allowing me a free visit to the *toilette.*

Returning to the bar, I studied the swank-looking cocktail-sipping Tropéziens. The clan with élan, the *belle clientèle*—a struggle ensued to put words to the scene before me.

"How would you describe the people here?" I asked Jean-Marc.

"Jet set."

"How else?"

"Refaits."

"That's not the word I'm looking for."

"Flashy."

"Don't you have a French word . . . like *vedette* or something?"

"Tape-à-l'œil."

With that, I think he hit it right on the—*head.*

REFERENCES: *une camionnette* (f) = small van; *le banc* (m) = bench; *ordinaire* = ordinary; *refait* = redone (surgically); *tape-à-l'œil* (from *taper à l'œil,* to hit the eye) = striking

270

Expressions

en vedette = in the limelight

une vedette de cinéma = a movie star

avoir la vedette = to be in the spotlight, in the headlines

jouer les vedettes = to act like a star

mettre en vedette = to put emphasis on, to put in evidence

ravir la vedette à quelqu'un = to steal the show from someone

partager la vedette = to share the limelight (with someone)

Vélo

(vay-lo)

noun, masculine

bike

En attente de mon homme. That is how I spent Sunday in the seaside town of Fréjus. Waiting, and waiting, and waiting for my man, who was taking part in a bike race. When he finally did surface, rounding the bend and waving an arm, he had mud on his face, and a very forced *sourire.*

"*C'est l'apocalypse. Ce n'est pas la peine de venir,*" he had said earlier when he called from the *Base Nature,* the former naval base in Fréjus.

My husband was in the fourth *vague,* or wave, as they say in race terminology, and would be departing a good hour and a half after the other *vététistes.* This turned out to be a stroke of *bonne chance,* for when the first racers left the *bloc de départ,* they were met with the said *apocalypse*—a violent rainstorm, heavy winds, and low visibility.

When a patch of blue sky surfaced here in Les Arcs, the kids and I raced to the car and headed south to the sea, eager to witness the twenty-first Roc d'Azur, touted as the biggest mountain biking *rassemblement* in the world.

After three hours camped alongside a canal, my eyes were blurry from studying so many *maillot*-clad, mud-faced mountain bikers. I still hadn't seen *le mien*. I remembered his getup: a black unitard and a black T-shirt. At the last minute he threw a white tank top over the black shirt. A goofy ensemble to be sure, but then his uniform might stand out from the sleek sponsored *maillots* that many of the other racers were wearing.

Finally he appeared, four hours and thirty minutes after that telephone call. He signaled with a weak wave of the arm and a pained smile on his face. My mouth flew open and out came a whoop that would have put Julia Roberts's character in *Pretty Woman* to shame: "*Whewwwwww Ewwwwww!!! Allleeeeeeeezzzzzzzzz!!!!!!!!!*"

"Hurry up!" I yelled to the kids, who had found an abandoned paddleboat with which to entertain themselves. "It's your papa!!!"

"*Allez, Papa!*" they screamed.

His brief appearance was worth the wait, and I am still amazed we managed to find him among the thirty-five hundred others who had signed up to participate in the fifty-five-kilometer race. The famous Roc 55 *parcours* began in 1984 with only seven competitors and a goal of riding "in harmony with nature." But from the looks of the *vététistes*, I'd say they were doing more battling with Dame Nature than harmonizing.

As for my own beat-up *vététiste*, next year I intend on pitching his leotard ensemble for something a little more *fringant*, and he'll need some flash next time (like a glittery pink ribbon for his helmet?) to stand out from the crowd.

REFERENCES: *C'est l'apocalypse. Ce n'est pas la peine de venir* = It's the apocalypse (here). No use coming; *vététiste* (m, f) = mountain biker; *la bonne chance* (f) = good luck; *le bloc de départ* (m) = starting block; *le rassemblement* (m) = gathering; *le mien* = mine; *le parcours* (m) = route; *fringant* = dashing

Viager

(vee-uh-zhay)

noun, masculine

rent for life

They are a little different," my husband warned as we drove into the parking lot.

The screen door opened and a man of a certain age appeared. Ink black ringlets fell to his shoulders. His roots were as white as his *chemise,* which was sheer and three quarters unbuttoned. A collection of gold chains glittered in the sun; tight white pants and three-inch platform heels completed his look. His wife wore a similar getup, only under her shirt, the trace of a sequined Wonderbra. Her waist-length hair was teased and tall; platinum blond wisps framed her face. Would-be rock stars at almost eighty.

We were meeting the couple who had put an announcement in the paper under *viager*—a not-so-uncommon real estate arrangement in which the buyer pays the seller a *bouquet,* or initial payment, and then a monthly fee for the duration of the seller's life, after which the buyer owns the property in full. (The seller usually remains on the property while collecting the *viager* fee.)

Madame pushed a tray of wrinkly black olives toward me before insisting on a tour of her seven-hundred-square-foot apartment. We navigated from room to room via handrails that were installed along all of the walls. A faux fireplace crackled in summertime, and a miniature waterfall (was that lava in the background?) flowed down one of the *salon* walls. Framed velvet wall art set the mood. I looked out the window: close to a dozen *nains de jardin* stared back.

Things got downright bizarre when Madame led us to her armoire. Inside, a dozen or so two-piece bathing suits stood up (from the padded brassiere cups); beyond, more rows of lingerie were neatly arranged.

"And the clothes, tell her she can have the clothes!" Madame shouted into Monsieur's ear. "These will be yours, all of them!"

275

We sealed the deal at the lawyer's office, where Monsieur expressed relief that we would be paying the monthly *viager* fee. I wanted him to know that this was not exactly my idea, that betting on his last breath was not in cadence with my morals. My husband and I had been thinking about an investment, as a way to save for retirement, and somehow stumbled onto the *viager* announcement . . . ironically enough.

No need to feel awkward, he assured us. His eight children had disowned him, and this *viager* arrangement was a welcome one—the monthly cash supplement would enable him and his second wife to live a bit more freely.

On the way out of the *notaire's* office, my husband suggested the four of us celebrate the transaction at the local café. Walking along the uneven cobblestone path, I leaped forward to assist when Monsieur became unbalanced, no thanks to his platform heels.

Our toast *fini*, I found it difficult bidding the couple farewell. What does one say? "So long"? (Not too long, we should hope . . .) "Take care"? (Just how sincere is that?) *"Adieu"*? (Presumptuous, *n'est-ce pas?*)

With a simple *"Au revoir,"* Monsieur and Madame eased into their convertible cherry red Mazda Miata and drove toward the sea, where the *coucher du soleil* kissed Mediterranean waters. *Ah, jeunesse!*

REFERENCES: *une chemise* (f) = shirt; *le nain de jardin* (m) = garden gnome; *le notaire* (m) = the lawyer (in real estate); *fini* = finished; *adieu!* (from *à Dieu*, to God) = farewell, good-bye forever; *le coucher du soleil* (m) = sunset; *la jeunesse* (f) = youth

Expressions

placer son argent en viager = to buy an annuity
mettre/acheter une maison en viager = to sell/buy a house in return for a life annuity

Voie

(vwah)

noun, feminine

lane

$\mathcal{A}$ single ascending road leads to *chez moi* from our medieval village. When I say single, I am referring to the *voie* (or lane). Not only is our *voie* single, it is superslight as well. If I am lucky, I'll make it to the top without the hindrance of a descending car, but more likely getting home requires a series of maneuvers including backing up, pulling into various driveways, and speeding forth before the next car descends.

When a car pulls over to let me pass, I smile behind the windshield, then mouth *"Merci, madame!"* or *"Merci, monsieur!"* with an affirmative nod; I think the gesture is more polite than flashing a hand.

If vehicles aren't there to obstruct, sheep are. Not long ago I sped up the path, thinking that I was home free, when a *troupeau* of *moutons* came meandering down the hill. I stopped my car in its tracks, rolled down the window, and let the grazers envelop the vehicle. The clanking collar bells and calls of the shepherd stopped time, if only for an instant.

REFERENCE: *un troupeau* (m) = flock

Expressions

préparer la voie = to prepare the way
sur la bonne voie = on the right track
en voie de = on the way to, in the process of
voie sans issue = dead end
voie ferrée = railway
voie publique = public highway
la Voie Lactée = the Milky Way

Volaille

(voh-lahy)

noun, feminine

fowl

While looking for a house in Saint-Maximin some years ago, the Realtor showed us the *cave* beneath the *rez-de-chaussée*, adding that the famous existentialist writer Albert Camus hid there during the Second World War. I noticed how she glanced sideways to check if we'd registered that bit of information. Of course, I wanted to believe her. *The Stranger* was a book I remember enjoying. Between Albert and the age of the house (over three hundred years!), I was beyond impressed.

For about the price of a brand-new Volkswagen sedan we bought that quirky and *étroit* village home, and soon settled into village life.

One chilly winter evening, I opened the *porte d'entrée* to find a stone-faced man dressed in fatigues and holding a pheasant.

The bird, almost as long as the man, now hung upside down,

dangling from its captor's extended arm. Either the *marchand de volailles* was making house calls or I was being offered a *petit cadeau*.

But how on earth to *plumer* a pheasant? My husband was out of town, and I was busy with my six-month-old baby girl and three-year-old Max. The last thing I needed was to dress and cook a pheasant (let alone pluck one); we were doing just fine on instant rice and canned ratatouille at that point.

The difficulty now was how to gracefully decline. I know that it is impolite to turn down a gift. I became nervous about disappointing my *voisin* by refusing this very original housewarming present.

Eventually I succeeded in declining, and the hunter was on his way. Off, I suppose, to court another village damsel in distress. Or one soon to be in distress!

280

REFERENCES: *la cave* (f) = cellar; *le rez-de-chaussée* (m) = ground floor; *étroit* = narrow; *la porte d'entrée* (f) = front door; *le marchand de volailles* = bird vendor; *un petit cadeau* (m) = little present

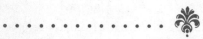

Also

foie de volaille = chicken liver
le volailler (la volaillère) = dealer in poultry and poultry
products, poulterer

Vouvoyer

(voo-voy-ay)

to address as "vous"

There's *tu* and then there's *vous*. *Moi,* I know that, or should by now. But in each of us there exists a little bit of revolution.

Yesterday was an unusually warm fall day and I didn't want to waste a second of it indoors. When the *maman* of Max's friend arrived to drop off her son for the afternoon, I invited her to stay for a cup of *café* and a chat *sous le soleil*. As we talked, I salt-and-peppered my phrases with *tu*. When it was my guest's turn to talk, she *vouvoyer*'d me, then each time excused herself: *"Dé-solée . . . tu . . ."*

I'm not 100 percent the bumbling American that I portray here; the 1 percent of me leftover knows better than to *tutoyer* a mere acquaintance. But I figured, We're almost the same age, we live in the country, and well, *pourquoi pas*?

Soon a tap dance of sorts ensued. My *invitée* would begin her sentences with *vous,* then change to *tu* midphrase, and I (sensing my guest to be ill at ease) would replace my *tu* with *vous*, until, in the end, we had somehow settled the matter.

Bidding her *au revoir*, I offered: *"Revenez. D'accord?"*

REFERENCES: *sous le soleil* = under the sun; *désolé(e)* = so sorry; *tutoyer* = to address as *"tu"*; *vous revenez (revenir)* = you come back now

. . . .

Also

vouvoyer quelqu'un = to address someone as *"vous"*

. . . .

Acknowledgments

*M*ille *mercis* to Ann Mah who put me in touch with Amanda Patten, my editor at Touchstone/Fireside. Thank you, Amanda, for making this book possible, for shaping it, and for bringing out the stories.

I am deeply grateful to Jean-Marc, Max, and Jackie for letting me write about them and for loving me and encouraging me throughout the process.

With loving thanks to my mom, Jules Greer, who thought I was funny and believed I could write. Thank you to my dad, Christopher Ingham, for the one-way ticket *back* to France, and for realizing, even before I did, just where I needed to be.

Special thanks to my sister, Heidi Stiteler, whose *esprit de famille* I appreciate and admire.

Thank you, Aunt Charmly and Uncle Tucker, for collecting my letters from the very beginning of this French experience, for enthusiastically reciting passages, and for your unwavering moral support.

Many thanks to my family and friends for their care and encouragement, especially: Audrey Marcus, Doug Stiteler, Marsha Ingham, Michèle-France Espinasse, Susan Boehnstedt, Dr. Howard Cutler, Kirsten Young, Barbara Barles, Chris White, Suzanne Serino, Corey Amaro, Brigitte Callegari, Fred Ingham, Claudia and Susunaga Weeraperuma, Cari and Pierre Casanova, and to friends and family whom I have not mentioned here, but who are as cherished as the lavender fields that surround Provence.

Sincères remerciements to Chris and George Christian, Kathy Tinoco, Liz Caughey, Alicia Weston, Donald Jackson, and Richard Patocchi for offering their editorial help on the original stories and asking nothing in return.

And, finally, *merci beaucoup* to French Word-A-Day readers, who have cheered me on, *and on.*